LET THERE BE LAUGHTER!

Jewish Humor in America

Let THere

JEWISH
HUMOR
IN
AMERICA

BE LAUGHTER!

ESTHER ROMEYN AND JACK KUGELMASS, CURATORS

 SPERTUS MUSEUM

Let There Be Laughter! Jewish Humor in America has been published on the occasion of the opening of the exhibition organized by Spertus Museum, Chicago.

Exhibition Curators
Esther Romeyn and Jack Kugelmass

Catalogue Design
Mike Brehm

Catalogue Cover Design
Tracy Kostenbader

Spertus Exhibition Staff
Mark Akgulian, Director of Design
Paula Chaiken, Assistant Curator of Education
Sheila Cronin, Exhibition Coordinator
Jim Dorling, Chief Exhibition Preparator
Tom Gengler, Chief Exhibition Registrar
Betsy Gomberg, Associate Museum Director
Dara Greenwald, Research Assistant
Tracy Kostenbader, Designer
Damon Locks, Research Assistant
Ellie Sandler, Director of Communications
Carole Silverstein, Research Assistant
Debbie Thornburg, Research Assistant
Olga Weiss, Curator of Exhibitions
Susan Schaalman Youdovin, Curator of Education
Azita Youssefi, Assistant Designer

ISBN 0-935982-54-X
Let There Be Laughter! Jewish Humor in America
Printed in Chicago
Spertus Institute of Jewish Studies is a beneficiary of the Jewish Federation of Metropolitan Chicago.

CONTENTS

"Some people say Ebenezer Scrooge is. But he's not. I'll tell you who is. All Three Stooges."
—Adam Sandler, "The Hanukkah Song"
Warner Bros., 1995. ProCD 7976

INTRODUCTION

A uniquely human form of expression, humor has long fascinated major thinkers, most notably Aristotle, Thomas Hobbes, Sigmund Freud, and Henri Bergson, each of whom developed a theory on the epistemology of laughter—or why it is that we find things funny. Freud's work is particularly significant because he used a number of Jewish jokes to illustrate his theories and in the process drew some important conclusions about the content of Jewish humor and the culture that spawned it.

From an ethnological standpoint, it would be hard to conceive of a culture without humor, or even one that does not value its own style of joking. But the idea that Jews have a *special* affinity to humor is ensconced in the popular imagination. Harry Golden writes that "Humor has been so much part of Jewish culture that any kind of activity at all is impossible without it."[1] Although there is ample reason to dispute that statement if we consider the broader trajectory of Jewish history, in America Jewish humor has attained unparalleled significance and visibility.

Humor's move to the center stage of Jewish culture can be attributed, in part, to the impact of Jewish mass migration from Eastern Europe and the ensuing process of acculturation. American Jewish humor bears the mark of a "double consciousness." It expresses the cultural incongruities that characterize the experience of a socially mobile group labeled as Other and determined to maintain a distinctive sense of self.

But the prominence of humor in American Jewish culture cannot be explained without also considering the substantial Jewish contribution to the development of the entertainment industry and the role of that industry in providing talented and ambitious Jews a route out of the ghetto. Long before Jews "invented Hollywood," they were active in vaudeville and Tin Pan Alley as performers and producers. Jews, according to the literary critic Leslie Fiedler, entered "American culture on the stage laughing."[2] The "comic Jew" has changed considerably since his first appearance on stage and in joke books a century ago. Initially endowed with an abundance of negative characteristics (particularly in regard to business ethics, morals, hygiene and physical attributes), the comic Jew has emerged as a paragon of virtue—the schlemiel as hero.[3]

More than just a ticket of entry into the host culture, for a large number of American Jews, humor has become a cornerstone of identity. It is a style of communication, of speaking and even thinking—in short, a coded language used by Jews to mark, perform and sometimes flaunt Jewish difference.[4]

The emergence of humor as a Jewish language on stage, in print, in sound, on screen, and in commodity culture is the subject of this exhibition.

THE NATURE OF JEWISH HUMOR

How Jewish?

The popular author Leo Rosten voices a commonly held belief when he asserts that "In nothing is Jewish psychology so vividly revealed as in the Jewish joke."[5] But this conception of Jewish humor as an essential characteristic of the Jewish spirit is relatively modern.[6] It originated in the late 19th century, when, with the rise of European nationalism, humor not only came to be regarded as a mark of civilization, but also was thought to embody the spirit of the *volk*, the people that formed the core of the emerging nation-state.

Seeking to identify themselves as a distinct and civilized nation, Jews were eager to prove that they, too, had a tradition of humor which captured the essence of the "Hebrew spirit."[7] Countering a commonly held opinion that denied "the Hebrew

3

race the faculty of laughter and the power of evoking laughter," Hermann Adler, the chief rabbi of London, in 1893, wrote

> **The Hebrews . . . at a comparatively early stage in their history, attained that ripe and strong mental development which the elaboration of wit and the comprehension of humour demand . . . .Crushed as he has been to the dust by the iron hand of bigotry, cowed by the soul-chilling venom of contempt and the oppression that "makest a wise man mad," he could not have survived, had not benign nature mercifully endowed him with extraordinary elasticity, with a wonderful power of resilience which enabled him to elude effectually all the attempts made at every age, and in every clime, to lay him down.[8]**

His article painted a continuous history of Jewish humor which stretched from witticisms of the Talmud and the Midrash, through the irreverence of the wandering preachers or *magidim,* to the wit of Heinrich Heine and Ludwig Börne.

In the United States, Abraham S. Isaacs' *Stories from the Rabbis* (1893) similarly sought to refute common perceptions of the Talmud as entirely other-worldly and humorless. In his introduction, Isaacs asserts that, although the Talmud is commonly believed to be the work of "mere dreamers . . . abstruse pedants dwelling in a solitary world of their own," in fact, it can boast its own share of "Fausts, Rip van Winkles and Baron Münchhausens."[9] A similar trajectory as the one outlined by Adler and Isaacs was emulated a decade later in Joseph

Chotzner's *Hebrew Humour and Other Essays* (1905) and its sequel, *Hebrew Satire* (1911).[10]

It was in these turn-of-the-century collections that the first conceptualizations of Jewish humor emerged. Jewish humor was interpreted through the prism of the Jewish experience, commonly viewed as a history of suffering and persecution. Indeed, given their history, the fact that Jews had humor at all testified to the special quality of Jewish laughter. According to Elliott Oring, it was in response to the question "why the Jew should laugh" that the main formulations which still dominate common perceptions about Jewish humor, were articulated. Jewish laughter was seen either as transcendent, philosophical, defensive or pathological.[11]

The most poignant formulation of Jewish humor as transcendent comes from the Yiddish author Sholem Aleichem's assessment of his own comic sensibility:

> **I tell you it is an ugly and mean world and only to spite it one musn't weep! If you want to know, that is the real source, the true cause of my constant good spirits, of my, as it is called, "humor." Not to cry out of spite! Only to laugh out of spite, *only to laugh.*[12]**

This view, later reformulated by others as "laughter through tears," asserts that East European Jewry survived the bitterness of its condition through self-mockery. Jewish humor is an expression of Judaism's messianic vision, which enabled Jews to transcend suffering and hold on to the hope of a better future.

Others argued that Jews used humor as a defensive, or even

retaliatory response to the oppressive conditions which they faced. Hermann Adler suggested that

> **The mirth of the Hebrew . . . is not the result of an over-abundance of animal spirits. It is not an outcome of the mere exuberance of being. I would rather liken it to the weapon with which a beneficent Maker has provided his feeble creatures, whereby they have been enabled to survive in the fierce struggle for existence.**[13]

Certainly the most noted commentator on Jewish jokes was Sigmund Freud. In *Jokes and Their Relation to the Unconscious*, which counts many Jewish jokes among its examples, Freud observed that he did "not know whether there are many other instances of a people making fun to such a degree of its own character."[14] This observation is the source of the widely held notion of the self-mocking nature of the Jewish joke. Building on Freud's ideas, some analysts (most notably Martin Grotjahn and Theodore Reik) have attributed a pathological dimension to such humor, considering it an expression of Jewish self-hatred.[15]

For some scholars, the "classic" Jewish joke is distinguished from more mundane humor by its philosophical dimension. As illustration, Richard Raskin cites the following joke from Immanuel Olsvanger's compilation of Yiddish humor, *Royte Pomerantsen*:

> **Two Jews have come to a rabbi to settle a legal dispute. Two dignified Jews with beard and earlocks, just as required. As usual, the rabbi's wife is also seated in the room. The rabbi says to one of the Jews: "So, what's your complaint?" He answers that the story is such and such, and he has to pay and he has to do this and he has to do that; in short, he gives such a fine account and argues his case so clearly that the rabbi has to say: "You're right." The rabbi then addresses the second Jew: "And what do you have to say?" The second Jew is nobody's fool either, and he also has a mouth to defend himself with; he argues his case so clearly that there is nothing left to be said, and that he owes nothing—not one cent. The rabbi says to him: "You're right." The rabbi's wife has never heard the likes of this and says to her husband: "You should live and be well! How can both of them be right? When one wins, the other has to lose." The rabbi says to his wife: "You're right, too."**

Raskin argues that the joke comprises three dimensions, which reside in the three possible explanations for the rabbi's behavior. They include: role fiasco—the rabbi is a bungling incompetent; tactical maneuver—the rabbi is a shrewd tactician; exemplary deviance—the rabbi's position is a philosophical statement about the ambiguity of reality. The coexistence of these three layers of meaning provides the key to the classic Jewish joke. It holds our attention through cognitive confusion: its meaning continually shifts as we consider each of the three dimensions.

Freud himself fondly quoted many *shadkhn* jokes as examples of the comic effects of faulty reasoning—jokes that exhibit the same kind of sophistry as many of the absurdist stories about the inhabitants of the Polish town of Chelm.

> A *shadchen* has brought an assistant with him to the discussion about the proposed bride, to bear out what he had to say. "She is straight as a pine-tree," said the *shadchen.*—"As a pine-tree," repeated the echo. —"And she has eyes that ought to be seen!"—"What eyes she has!" confirmed the echo.—"And she is better educated than anyone!" —"What an education!" —"It's true that there's one thing," admitted the broker, "she has a small hump." —"And *what* a hump!" the echo confirmed once more.

> The bridegroom was paying his first visit to the bride's house in the company of the broker, and while they were waiting in the salon for the family to appear, the broker drew attention to a cupboard with glass doors in which the finest set of silver was displayed. "There! Look at that! You can see from these things how rich these people are." —"But," asked the suspicious young man, "mightn't it be possible that these fine things were only collected for the occasion —that they were borrowed to give an impression of wealth?" —"What an idea!" answered the broker protestingly. "Who do you think would lend these people anything?"[16]

Running through all these interpretations is the idea that Jewish jokes are of a rather intellectual nature. But the repertoire of Jewish humor includes much more mundane humor as well. Dialect humor, Jewish mother jokes and so-called "J.A.P." (Jewish-American Princess) jokes can be particularly mean-spirited. Scatological and sexual jokes were just as much a part of the humor of the shtetl as the Borscht Belt. The traditional jesters and jokesters of East European Jewry, the *marshalik* and *badkhn*, were known for their ribaldry and lewd suggestions, and feared for their parodies of fellow townspeople. Indeed, the *badkhn's* humor lent itself to secular reinterpretation and became a standard sketch of 20th-century Yiddish comedians such as Benny Bell[17] and Leo Fuchs.[18] Jennie Goldstein, the "Yiddish Comedienne," parodied the tradition by inflecting a typical *badkhn* routine from a woman's perspective:

> Oy, cry *kale lebn* [dear bride] cry, cry, cry! Your girl-hood days, you can kiss goodbye.
> Remember carefully what I have to say,
> 'Cause you won't be tomorrow what you are today.[19]

Moreover, one would be hard put to identify any joke as uniquely Jewish. Indeed, sometimes, a simple change of names and place enable jokes to cross cultural boundaries, as the following joke illustrates:

> A Jew survives a shipwreck on a desert island. Years later he is rescued by a passing ship and he escorts the captain around his compound. First he shows his house and garden and at the end of the tour the lovely synagogue he built. "If this is your synagogue," the captain inquires, "then what's that building over there?" "Oh, that?" the rescued man replies, "That's the *shul* I don't go to."

Although the joke is often cited as an illustration of the Jewish penchant for disagreements, it appears with a slight change of details (including a chapel rather than a synagogue) in a collection entitled *Welsh Jokes*![20]

Ultimately, any attempt to define the unique characteristics of the "classic" Jewish joke, and through it obtain a window to some eternal Jewish spirit, is bound to fail. There are, however, factors which may have stimulated a Jewish penchant for humor, and it is our contention that tracing this penchant offers a more productive route to understanding the special nature of Jewish humor.

A dominant strategy of humor in general, as Elliott Oring explains, is the establishment of "an appropriate interrelationship of domains that are generally regarded as incongruous in a particular frame."[21] But the range of inconsistent domains or circumstances available may vary among different groups. Historical, social, and cultural factors may have sensitized Jews to incongruity. Rabbinic discourse is noted for its frequent validation of contradictory opinions. Moreover, Jewish experience throughout the Diaspora was characterized by internal bilingualism. Jews inhabited a world in which they switched between two or more linguistic codes (Yiddish or Ladino and Hebrew in addition to the local non-Jewish vernacular), which resulted in a strong predisposition towards linguistic play and cultural punning.

This sensitivity to the ambiguities of meaning took on added significance after the Enlightenment (beginning among Jews in Western Europe around the mid 18th century). Eager to participate in society at large, Jews increasingly experienced the world bi-culturally. Mastering the habits of bourgeois life, they became distanced from their native culture, but at the same time some considered it a refuge from the strictures of their adopted culture.[22] Navigating two (or more) cultures simultaneously, and looking at themselves through the eyes of the dominant group, Jews developed what the turn-of-the-century scholar W.E.B. du Bois, referring to the plight of African Americans, called a "double consciousness," borne out of an existence on the margins of a society which simultaneously demands that a group assimilate to its standards while labeling its members as Other.[23] It is this predicament—which became even more pronounced in the wake of the mass migration of Jews from Eastern Europe to America—that engenders ethnic laughter.[24]

JEWISH HUMOR AS ETHNIC HUMOR[25]

After noting the remarkable number of self-critical jokes which "have grown up on the soil of Jewish popular life," Freud took pains to distinguish the self-deprecating element in Jewish humor from Gentile jokes about Jews:

> The jokes made about Jews by foreigners are for the most part brutal comic stories in which a joke is made unnecessary by the fact that Jews are regarded by foreigners as comic figures. The Jewish jokes which originate from Jews admit this, too; but they know their real

faults as well as the connection between them and their good qualities, and the share which the subject has in the person found fault with creates the subjective determinant . . . of the joke-work.[26]

Conceptually, Freud was trying to establish the difference between the self-directed element in Jewish humor, and Jewish jokes as told by members of the dominant group. But his distinction creates neat boundaries where, in reality, lines are blurred. As many scholars have observed, the same joke told by different performers to different audiences, or in different contexts, can have radically different meanings.

This issue is central to any discussion of the place of Jewish humor in American culture. The fact that "Jews entered American culture on the stage laughing," contains all the ambiguities that were inherent in "crossing over." The development of the entertainment industry in general, and the humor business in particular, for many Jewish immigrant children provided a way out of the ghetto. But it was as comic types—in portrayals that sometimes invoked the most negative Jewish stereotypes—that Jews first gained entry, and consequently, visibility in American popular culture. In these performances, which derived their laughter from allusions to the Jews' physical appearance, convoluted language, and questionable business ethics, the line between affectionate self-parody and the performance of negative stereotype, between laughing with, or laughing at, was hard to draw.[27]

Indeed, the prevalence of the comic Jew as a stage type

(more often than not performed by Jewish comedians) stimulated campaigns to rid the stage and screen of "anti-Jewish stereotypes" and substitute them with more "authentic" Jewish representations. Jewish comedians entertaining non-Jewish, or mixed audiences with jokes about their fellow Jews were accused of internalizing the biases of the majority culture. But what such campaigns failed to notice was that Jewish comedians frequently inflected these stereotypes with their own comic voices. In doing so, they were able to transform older stage conventions into vehicles for Jewish self-expression.

Like all ethnic humor, American Jewish humor contains various codes or inflections which often go unnoticed by, or are unintelligible to, out-group audiences, but radically affect its meaning. In the following section, we outline four principal modalities of ethnic humor. Each suggests another level of complexity; combined, they reveal just how serious humor is for the culture that performs it.

1) ETHNOGRAPHY

Ethnic joking performances may be seen as vehicles for microsociological analyses that groups perform upon themselves, upon others, and upon problems of pressing concern. But ethnic humor also has its own symbolic economy: it relies upon highly coded and simplified typologies of the in-group, subgroups within the in-group, as well as of the various out-groups, to perform such analyses.

This tendency toward stereotyping of Self and Other is especially pronounced during times of rapid social change, or when cultures are in contact for the first time. Although often met with strong opprobrium (it certainly violates contemporary standards of intercultural etiquette), such stereotyping, rather than debasing the ethnic Self or dehumanizing the ethnic Other, may help ethnic groups understand and adjust to a new cultural environment. While ethnic humor often replicates the prevailing hierarchies of race, ethnicity, gender and class, it may also create a space for the positive assertion of difference by making cultural and linguistic peculiarities seem more like harmless quirks than loathsome habits.

2) TRAVESTY

If one aspect of ethnic humor reveals its rootedness within a particular social and cultural context, another concerns its potential to liberate. Freud suggested that sometimes humor does nothing more than offer temporary release from the strictures of social and cultural proprieties.[28] Others are less convinced about the innocuousness of such release. Racist and sexist jokes may simply offer their tellers a means to mask officially proscribed prejudice ("it's only a joke").[29] But many scholars recognize in humor's topsy-turviness culture's *Spielraum* (play realm). Through inversion, parody and incongruity we gain the capacity to imagine alternate ways of constructing reality. Indeed, without that capacity cultures would become hopelessly ossified.[30]

Humor creates utter havoc with the world as we know it, and it accomplishes this on two separate axes. On a vertical plane travesty turns high into low, respectability into disrepute; on a horizontal plane it continually transposes cultural categories (such as gender, denomination, class) and subverts intercultural boundaries—the Yiddish speaking Indians of Eddie Cantor's *Whoopee* and Mel Brooks's *Blazing Saddles*, or Fanny Brice's "Yiddishe Squaw" Rosie Rosenstein.

Although travesty is an important element in all ethnic humor, 70 years ago the cultural critic Gilbert Seldes recognized it as a particularly Jewish comic code. Characterizing the performances of two comedians, Al Jolson and Fanny Brice, as "daemonic," Seldes wrote:

It is noteworthy that these two stars bring something to America which America lacks and loves—they are, I suppose, two of our most popular entertainers—and that both are racially out of the dominant caste. Possibly this accounts for their fine carelessness about our superstitions of politeness and gentility. The medium in which they work requires more decency and less frankness than usually exist in our private lives; but within these bounds Jolson and Brice go farther, go with more contempt for artificial notions of propriety, than anyone else.[31]

More recently, the critic Irving Howe characterized the work of the Marx Brothers in a similar vein:

In their films the disassembled world is treated with total disrespect, an attitude close to the traditional feeling among Jews that the whole elaborate structure of gentile power is merely trivial. The gleeful nihilism of the Marx Brothers made a shamble of things, reducing their field of operations to approximately what a certain sort of East Side skeptic had always thought the world to be: *ash un porukh*, ashes and dust.[32]

According to Stephen Whitfield, this dimension of Jewish humor evinces "its uneasy but discernable relation to the idea of culture itself, especially high culture." Jewish popular entertainers are part of an ethnic group that prides itself on intellectual abilities.

As involuntary heirs to a formidable tradition of learning, they were naturally alert to the comic possibilities inherent in their own diminished stature. Playing in the tackiest rooms in the house of intellect, the comedians made such incongruities pivotal to their craft and even on occasion to their sensibility and vision.[33]

In their performances, they assaulted the aura of high culture, and exerted their own claims of cultural ownership by inflecting the high with their own, "low" perspective.

This apotheosis of the low suggests the deeper meaning of ethnic travesty. As a comic strategy, it not only *decenters* its own frame of reference, the standards of the majority culture and what it designates as "high" culture. It simultaneously carves out a niche within a major language, which it speaks and "writes" in a minority's voice—an example of what literary scholars Gilles Deleuze and Felix Guattari describe as *reterritorialization*.[34]

Perhaps that is why musical instruments, as symbols of artistic aspiration, have been a favorite comic prop of Jewish comedians (Jack Benny, Victor Borge, Harpo and Chico Marx and Henny Youngman, to name only a few).[35] But the assault on the high is by no means limited to music. American mythology (the West in particular), literature, as well as art have long been favorite targets of Smith and Dale, Woody Allen, Mel Brooks and Neil Simon. But Jewish laughter's most radical decentering occurs in regard to language. From the early days of dialect comedy to such modern television sitcoms and "dramadies" as *Mad About You*, *The Nanny*, and *Northern Exposure*, Jewish comedians have inflected the language of the majority culture with their own, low vernacular. A particularly good example is Mickey Katz's use of Yiddish/Yinglish to render popular American songs Jewish. A generation later, Allan Sherman used a simple change in names, situations and syntax to do the same. A hilarious example is his rendition of *"Frère Jacques:"*

Sarah Jackman, Sarah Jackman
How's by you? How's by you?
How's by you the family?
How's your sister Em'ly?
She's nice too.
She's nice, too.[36]

The song became such an overnight hit when Allen Sherman's *My Son the Folksinger* was released that the guests in the lobby of a New York hotel could hear President Kennedy singing it as he headed towards a waiting limousine.[37]

3) SATIRE: HUMOR AS A WEAPON OF THE WEAK

Various scholars have discerned an aggressive impulse underlying wit. Although humor often targets the weak (hence the popularity of ethnic, racial and gender slurs), it also offers a relatively safe way to attack the powerful. Consider this example from a collection of Soviet emigré jokes:

> Abraham telephoned the KGB.
> "Hello. Is this the KGB headquarters? I was just wondering whether by any chance a parrot has come to your office," Abraham inquired.
> "No," came the reply.
> "Well, if he should come, I just want to let you know in advance that I don't share his political views," Abraham explained.[38]

These jokes went beyond the in-group confines and became a vehicle for Soviet citizens to mediate the gap between official discourse and actual experience.[39]

Humor was also an important part of resistance during the Nazi period for all peoples, including Jews in ghettos and camps.[40] But even when there is no significant danger, humor gives its users the satisfaction of besting the majority culture and its allures. Take the following:

> Three converts to Episcopalianism are drinking together in their ritzy country club, when they begin explaining the reasons for their switch from Judaism.
> "I converted out of love," the first one said. Seeing the dubious looks on his friends' faces, he added, "Not for Christianity but for a Christian girl. As you know, my wealthy wife insisted that I convert."
> "And I converted in order to succeed in law," the second one said. "I would never have been appointed a federal judge if I hadn't become an Episcopalian."
> "I converted because I think that the teachings of Christianity are superior to those of Judaism," the third one said.
> "Whom are you trying to kid?" the first man answered with considerable heat. "What do you take us for—a couple of goyim?"[41]

4) SELF-SATIRE

Self-critical humor is not necessarily pathological or a mark of self-hatred. It can, in fact, serve to affirm cultural identity and reinforce group boundaries. And it can do so in the following ways:

a) Social levelling: According to Freud, one effect of the self-deprecating character of Jewish humor is the privileging of ethnic inclusiveness over social distinctions. As an example, he cited the following joke:

> A Galician Jew was travelling in a train. He had made himself really comfortable, had unbuttoned his coat and put his feet up on the seat. Just then a gentleman in modern dress entered the compartment. The Jew promptly pulled himself together and took up a proper pose. The stranger fingered through the pages of a notebook, made some calculations, reflected for a moment and then suddenly asked the Jew: "Excuse me, when is Yom Kippur (the Day of Atonement)?" "Oho!" said the other Jew, and put his feet back on the seat before answering.

b) Cultural lag: While such jokes can criticize the pretensions of upwardly mobile parvenu Jews or *allrightniks* (Jews who have embraced the values and customs of the host culture), and pull them back into the fold, self-ridicule can also promote change, particularly during periods of significant social and economic mobility. In dialect humor and greenhorn jokes, the imitation of the speech patterns, gestures and mannerisms of the immigrant lets a succeeding generation celebrate its attainment of cultural proficiency at the expense of its elders.[42]

> A young Jewish couple from New York decides they want to go to Florida for a vacation, but the hotel they want to stay at is restricted. The man tells his wife he thinks it will work out and they will be able to stay at the hotel just as long as she doesn't open her mouth, because nobody will know they are Jewish. So they make the trip, and everything goes just fine. They check into the hotel, and the wife never opens her mouth. They go up to their room and pretty soon the wife decides she would like to take a swim. The husband tells her to go ahead but reminds her not to say anything. So she goes down to the pool for her swim. She sticks her toe into the water and it is just terribly cold, and she yells out, "Oi vey!" Then, looking around, horrified, she adds, "Wat ever dat means."[43]

c) Ethnic mirroring: Ethnic humor frequently inverts negative stereotypes and turns them into positive symbols of collective identity. As a result, ethnic humor may construct collective selfhood in carnivalesque terms—as vulgar, loud, given to excess, or unsophisticated—but invest these stereotypes with a positive meaning. Validating outsiders' stereotypical images of the group grates against some ethnic nerves, but others are well disposed towards this kind of characterization, particularly when generated or performed by members of the group itself. Stereotypes defiantly reassert group autonomy even in the face of significant social mobility and cultural assimilation by declaring, "This is the way we are, the way we have always been and the way we always will be!" A joke performed by Mickey Katz to illustrate this point:

> "You know a fellow came home the other night . . . and he says, "*Oys* [no longer] Jew!"

He says, "I'm going to become an Episcopalian."

She says, "*Mit aza pisk* [with such a face], an Episcopalian?"

He says, "I'm gonna get *geshmadt* [converted] and that's all."

She thinks he's crazy. She lets him go about his way. He comes back later and says, "*Shoyn geshmadt* [already converted]. Not a Jew anymore. And you're just a Jewish woman that vorks in mine house. Don't talk to me unless I talk to you."

She wakes up the next morning. She goes in his room, she sees he's got his *talis* on, *tfilin*, and he's *shokln* [rocking], his yarmulke *un er davnt un er shoklt azoy dortn* [and he's praying and rocking]. She says, "I thought you weren't a Jew anymore?"

And he looks around and says, "How do you like that? *Goyishe kop* [non-Jewish head]!"[44]

HUMOR IN TRADITIONAL JEWISH CULTURE
From Bible to Folk Culture

Historically, humor was neither particularly characteristic of Jewish culture, nor did it suffuse any of the great texts upon which Judaism is built. But scholars have noted various instances of humor in the Bible: Sarah's laughter when God informs her of an imminent birth despite advanced age, and her choice of the name for her newborn son, Itzhak, or Isaac, meaning "he who laughed;" the Book of Esther, with its inversions of status and deep sense of irony such as when King Ahasverus asks, "What shall be done unto the man whom the king delighteth to honour," and his minister, Haman, assuming he is the one to be favored by the king, provides a list of appropriate marks of royal honor, which are subsequently bestowed upon his arch enemy, Mordechai.[45] But these examples notwithstanding, compared to the literature of classical Greece

Knopf. 249 E. Houston St.

Der Vortrag des Marschelik. (Spassmacher)

דער מארשאלעק ביים טיש תורה זאגען

Der marshalik baym tish toyre zogn. The marshalik (jester) entertains the wedding guests with a parodic homily. (YIVO Archives)

and Rome, the classical literature of the Jews is not very funny. Consequently, some scholars suggest that the roots of Jewish mirth are to be found in Talmudic casuistry and Midrash:

> **When the thief lacks opportunity he is condemned to honesty. (Sanh. 22a)[46]**
>
> **If one person tells thee thou hast asses' ears, do not mind it; but if two persons make this assertion, at once place a saddle-sack upon thy back.[47]**

Humor, however, was generally regarded suspiciously by Jewish religious leaders in medieval Europe, afraid that levity would promote lecherous behavior. Secular entertainments such as theater or festivals were not tolerated. Despite religious injunctions, humorous parables figured prominently in the repertoire of wandering preachers or *magidim*. Moreover, communities seized upon one of the few forms of communal recreation, the wedding, as an occasion for humorous release.

As early as the 13th century, merrymakers, who were grudgingly tolerated by the rabbinate because of their popularity, amused wedding guests with parodies and songs. Jewish jesters were known under various terms, according to their specialties: A *leyts* (jester) signified a comedian or satirist, who could also be a musician; the *marshalik* acted as a master of ceremonies during the Middle Ages, but took on a more typical clown character in the 17th century, when local or state bans on large celebrations made the ceremonial role redundant; his competitor, the *badkhn,* was the "intellectual" of the traditional Jewish jesters, and he often assumed the guise of a popular moralizer, who interpolated his satirical homiletics with Talmudic passages[48].

The holiday of Purim presented an annual occasion for comic license. Jews sometimes donned costumes, and performed *purimshpiln* (Purim plays), which dramatized the story of Esther or relevant biblical stories, but would often include satires of sacred and secular Jewish institutions, parodies of rabbinical arguments or prayers, and caricatures of prominent people within the community.[49] The *purimshpiln* and related parodies continue to be a vital tradition in contemporary Hasidic communities. But the holiday, with its opportunities for parodies, plays and costuming, appeals to other religious and secular Jews as well.

Jewish folk culture also had a strong tradition of humorous lore. European Jewry in particular engendered a genre of humorous folk narratives featuring archetypal droll types. Typically, such folk characters as *schnorrers* (cheapskates), *schlemiels* or *shlimazls* (characteristically luckless and inept), and *luftmentshn* (other-worldly schemers or those without any apparent means of subsistence) functioned not just as comic foils, but lent themselves to parodies of religious zealotry, social ambitions and codes of respectability.

The best known folk narratives are the Chelm stories, non-

זוכען גאָלדענע אוצרות.

Zukhn goldene oytsres [Looking for golden treasures]. The wise men from Chelm mistake a water lily for gold. *Khelmer khakhomim* [The Wise Men of Chelm]. Illustrations by Evelyn Blumgarden. (New York: Hebrew Publishing Company, 1933) (Kugelmass Collection)

sense tales about the Jewish inhabitants of the Polish town of Chelm, which mock the self-absorption and other-worldliness of the Talmudic scholar. The narratives typically take logic to the extreme. When confronted with a problem, the Chelmites suggest a solution that is theoretically correct but practically absurd.[50]

Two sages of Chelm went out for a walk. One carried an umbrella, the other didn't.

Suddenly, it began to rain.

"Open your umbrella, quick!" suggested the one without an umbrella.

"It won't help," answered the other.

"What do you mean, it won't help? It will protect us from the rain."

"It's no use, the umbrella is as full of holes as a sieve."

"Then why did you take it along in the first place?"

"I didn't think it would rain."[51]

A Chelmite at a bright street corner looks for a coin he has lost. "Did you drop it here?" he is asked. "No, I dropped it back there in the dark, but it's easier to look for it here by the light."[52]

Some tales about mischief makers and trickster types were based on real people. Hershele Ostropoler, a legendary comic character, was born in the Ukraine around 1750. According to legend, he lost his job as *shoykhet* (ritual slaughterer) as a result of his continuous joking, but was eventually hired by a melancholic Hasidic rabbi as court jester.[53] His counterpart, Motke Chabad, the most famous jester of Lithuania, earned his living as a *badkhn*. Hershele Ostropoler and Motke Chabad are archetypal fools who survive by their wits and triumph over misfortune through their absurd reinterpretations of apparently disadvantageous situations, in the process indicting the rich and powerful.

Once a fire broke out in the house where Motke Chabad was living. As the house went up in flames, the inhabitants all rushed outside in a frenzy. Some brought pails of water, but Motke stood there laughing. "What are you laughing at?" they asked him. Motke replied: "I see my revenge on the cockroaches."[54]

HUMOR AND THE JEWISH ENLIGHTENMENT

The Social Dimension

It was probably not until after the Jewish Enlightenment that Jewish humor developed its characteristic self-reflexive irony. In Germany, the life of Heinrich Heine exemplifies the ambiguities implicit in the novel position Jews came to occupy. Heine was born in 1797 in Düsseldorf into a traditional Orthodox family. He later converted to Protestantism in order to procure an academic position, but conveyed his cynical perspective towards Christianity in his witticism about the baptismal certificate as "the passport of entry into European culture."[55]

Credited with introducing Jewish humor to German literature, Heine's biting irony specifically targets religious hypocrisy and the pretensions of class and nobility. One of his characters was the lottery agent and extractor of corns, Hirsch Hyazinth, who boasts: "and, as true as God shall grant me all good things, Doctor, I sat beside Solomon Rothschild and he treated me quite as an equal, quite famillionairely."[56]

During the later decades of the nineteenth century, the Enlightenment movement or *Haskalah* gained an increasing influence among East European Jews. Inspired by the results of the Emancipation in Germany and France, and full of optimism that the authorities would be favorably disposed toward modernized Jews, *maskilim* or Jewish enlighteners advocated a complete make-over of the shtetl Jew—the adoption of western dress, and the learning of the local, non-Jewish vernaculars and trades. In their hands humor became a weapon to ridicule outmoded customs and traditions.

The early work of Mendele Mokher Sforim, the pseudonym of Sholem Abramovitch (1836-1917), showed the influence of the *Haskalah* in its orientation toward social satire. His most famous work, *Neseyes Binyomin Hashlishi*, or *The Travels of Benjamin III* (1878), however, expresses Mendele's increasing disillusionment with the premises of self-help and education on which the *Haskalah* was built. Moving away from social satire, the novel embraces the same folk irony that generated the stories of Chelm and Hershele Ostropoler.[57]

The most widely recognized writer to emerge from this period was Sholem Aleichem (1859–1916). In his humorous tales about the mythical town of Kasrilevke, the *kleyne mentshelekh* (little people) of the shtetl inhabit their own version of reality, which denies the indignities and humiliations of daily life. Choosing faith over skepticism, the people of Kasrilevke, such as Tevye, the dairyman, maintain an ironic dialogue with God. Another favorite Sholem Aleichem character is Menakhem Mendl, a Jack-of-all-trades, who fails in a long list of occupations—investor, stockbroker, real estate agent, insurance agent, marriage broker and undertaker. His is the voice of the *luftmentsh*, the man without any particular skills, occupation, or capital, who tries to make a living by his wits. Undisturbed by any self-reflexivity, Mendl transforms every failure into a private success. [58]

If, in the declining economy of Eastern Europe in the latter 19th century, the *luftmentsh* represented a sizable percentage of the population, by the time of his writing, shtetl life as Sholem Aleichem projected it was already a nostalgic image. Industrialization, impoverishment, political oppression and persecution had forced many Jews from villages and small towns into larger cities in Europe and America. Indeed, Sholem Aleichem himself briefly resettled in New York City at the turn of the century. As a playwright molded in the Old World, in America he never achieved the success he aspired to. Disillusioned, he returned to Europe, only to be exiled once again in the aftermath of World War I. But his tales of the people of Kasrilevke, brought to the New World by Jewish immigrants, became emblematic of the shtetl they left behind, and of Jewish persistence in the face of adversity.

Sholem Aleichem's failure as an American artist at the beginning of the century stands in marked contrast to his impact on American Jewish culture. Widely popularized through translations and Broadway and Hollywood productions, his stories have not only shaped the image of shtetl life, and influenced common perceptions of "classic" Jewish humor, but they have also left their mark on succeeding generations of American Jewish writers and comics. One critic recently detected the influence of Sholem Aleichem in the popular television series, "Sergeant Bilko." Like Tevye, Bilko has a continuing (if not exactly devout) dialogue with God. In episode after episode, he raises his eyes to heaven and voices a heartfelt appeal, usually when, to his great dismay, his conscience has sabotaged his "better," that is, his greedy instincts. Sholem Aleichem happened to be the favorite author of the show's creator, Nat Hiken. [59]

IMMIGRATION

The Humor of Self-Transformation

The transition from the Old to the New World constituted an experience of extreme displacement. Dreams of America as *di goldene medine* gave way—at least during this early period of immigration—to a reality of poverty and struggle. In a continuation of the satiric tradition of the *Haskalah* and Old World socialism, Jewish immigrants vented their disillusionment through parody. One example is Gerson Rosenzweig's *Talmud Yankai* (*Yankee Talmud*), first published in 1907. On pages that resemble those of a religious tractate, Rosenzweig directs his sarcasm at the high and the low, the peddler, the teacher and the rabbi, while denouncing the vulgarities of the New World, its love of money, spiritual emptiness, and worship of success.[60]

But the sense of social and cultural alienation, of living

דער גרויסער קונדס

מעטעמארפאזע נומער 5

אין דער היים האט ער אָנגעטריבען אַ פערד און וואָגען

— און דאָ, טרײבט ער אָן איין אָרקעסטער.

In der heym hot er getribn a ferd un vogn—un do, traybt er on an orkester [In the old country he drove a horse and wagon—here he leads an orchestra] "Metamorfosen 5," *Der groyser kundes* (July 2, 1909) (YIVO Library)

between two worlds, also gave rise to a new form of Jewish humor which played upon the cultural incongruity, status reversals, and generational conflicts experienced by Jewish immigrants. The overwhelming sense of the topsy-turviness of the New World is perhaps best illustrated by the cartoon series "*Metamorfosen*" ("Metamorphoses") which the humorous Yiddish weekly *Der groyser kundes* (*The Big Stick*) ran in 1909. One of the captions reads:

In America, the former coachman has become a conductor.

Another:

The teacher, who in Poland taught the children Talmud, in America learns English from his pupils.

Similar conflicts were also dramatized in cartoons and newspapers, songs and recordings, on the contemporary Yiddish stage, and somewhat later, in Jewish films. One popular song, *"Vos ken yu makh, es iz Amerike*!" ("What Can You Do, It's America!"), originally performed by Aaron Lebedeff in the comic operetta, *Litvisher Yankee,* humorously reflects:

What can you do?—It's America!
The Jews here look the same as the non-Jews.
Here in America, everything's backwards—
Men shave, and women grow beards!
What can you do?—It's America![61]

Yiddish vaudeville was particularly sensitive to the new environment. Emerging in the last years of the 19th century in the saloons of the Lower East Side, it shared many of the characteristics of American vaudeville. As its popularity grew, it changed venues, moving first into music halls and then into lavishly decorated theaters. Songs made famous by popular actors were recorded and published as sheet music, and reached an even wider public.

With comic stock types such as the *griner (*the greenhorn), the *allrightnik* (who adopts all the customs of the new country),

the peddler, the butcher, the cantor, and the *schlemiel* husband with his domineering wife, the popular Yiddish stage presented, in burlesque form, an index of the immigrants' social world. But their exaggerated mannerisms, ill-fitting clothing, and convoluted speech patterns also mirrored the immigrants' feelings of linguistic clumsiness and cultural ineptness.

The distinguishing feature of this New World humor is the importance of dialect. The continuous switching between Yiddish, English and "Yinglish" is indicative of the ways in which this humor functions as a site for reflection on the problems of cultural self-definition. The nature of this reflection, however, changed continually. Early Yiddish vaudeville often exploited ethnic in-group differences. The song *"Der Litvak un der Galitsianer"* (1914), for example, evoked the regional differences in Yiddish dialect and the misinterpretations resulting from inter-regional contact and marriage. The song was a standard act for generations of Yiddish vaudevillians, including Lee Tully:

From my wife, I get such aggravation, she's driving me out of my wits,
She's from a different denomination, I'm a *Litvak* and she's a *Galits*.
We're happily married, I don't want to squawk,
We understand each other completely, except when we talk.
I say *"mutter"*[mother], she says *"mitter,"*
Es iz mir biter[it disturbs me] *ikh zog* [I say] *"putter"* [butter], she says *"pitter,"*

What's the difference, *mutter, mitter, pitter*? Oy, how I
shvits,
'Cause I'm a *Litvak* and she's a *Galits*.[62]

Differences between Jews from the Ukraine, Lithuania and
Poland also received parodic treatment. A Leo Fuchs sketch, for
example, featured a comical interpretation of the different
dancing styles of a *Ukrainer*, a *Litvak*, and a *Polak*.

But it was in the intersection of Yiddish with American cul-
ture(s), that Jewish humor fashioned its own voice. Comic
sketches and songs with titles such as "*Galitsianer Caballero*,"
"*Litvisher* Yankee," "Scotchman from Orchard Street" or "Cordova, the Bronx Casanova" indicate the adoption, in Yiddish
vaudeville, of ethnic pastiche, a form of cultural cross-fertil-
ization which was already well developed in American popular
theater.[63] Consisting of the coupling of two incongruous cultural domains, cultural pastiche, as Ronald Sanders suggests,
"is a gift of peoples who live in ambivalent situations."[64] Such
pastiche creates linguistically and culturally layered texts, as
illustrated by Leo Fuchs's "*Yiddisher* Cowboy," a musical parody
of the American popular song "Home on the Range" in which
the Wild West is replaced by the Catskills resorts and the "cowboy" turns out to be a notorious womanizer:

Menashe Skulnik as "The Scotchman from Orchard Street"
(Peter H. Schweitzer Collection)

I'm Leybke, the Yiddishe Cowboy, *ikh shray* [I scream]
"Yip-i aye, ain't that mellow,"
I've been through the mill, and I know every hill,
From Mountaindale, to Monticello.
Home, home on the Range . . .
I know every bush *vu men khapt arayn a kush* [where
you can grab a kiss].
Un ikh khap arayn nokh epes oykh [and I grab some-
thing else too].

In a play on dialect comedy, characters would suddenly lapse into cultural mannerisms and speech—including "Indian" and "Black" inflected Yiddish—that are not of their own group. [65] Cultural pastiche and ventriloquism (the speaking of one's own ethnic voice while wearing the mask of another) went on to become common strategies in Jewish comedic performances, including those of Fanny Brice, Eddie Cantor, Sam Levenson, Mel Brooks, Sid Caesar, Allan Sherman and many others.

Another strategy that still dominates American Jewish humor is the comic use of Yiddish. In the 1920s and '30s, as immigrant audiences became acculturated, Yiddish vaudeville made increasing use of "potato Yiddish." This parody of the malapropisms and fractured language of first-generation Jewish immigrants in effect transformed Jewish vaudeville into bi-lingual comedy, and gave it considerable appeal to second-generation audiences. [66] Mickey Katz specialized in musical and linguistic parodies in songs such as *The Ballad of Duvid Crock-*

ett (The King of Delancey Street)," "*Heym afn reyndzh* (Home on the Range)," and "*Geshray af di vilde katshke* (The Wild Goose's Scream)". Although Katz's music was considered too Jewish for commercial radio, and even for some Jewish audiences, "Tickle, Tickle," a version of the popular Latin American melody "*Tico, Tico*," made him an instant hit in the Mexican-American communities of Los Angeles.

Masters of the art of bi-lingual comedy, the Barton Brothers combined music and off-color humor to tease their Americanized public.

Oy, tsuris, oy, tsuris [Problems, oy, problems].
Keyner hot nit mer [No one has more of them than I].
Oyb tsuris volt geveyn gelt [If only problems were money],
Bin ikh a milyoner [I'd be a millionaire].
"Hey, Lucky!"
"What, I'm lucky? I come home from work and find my wife with another man in the living room. As soon as she sees me she says, "Quick! Hayim, go upstairs and make me coffee!"
"Did you make coffee for him, too?"
"To hell with him! Let him make his own coffee!"[67]

The lyrics of some female performers were much more sardonic. Jennie Goldstein's "*Ikh hob zikh gelozt* [I gave in]," the comic-tragic indictment of a young woman whose unguarded moment has left her an unwedded mother of triplets, reveals the dark side of romance. But her "Platinum Fox" which reflects on Jewish social mobility as well as gender politics is a comedic masterpiece:

> "Oh wait a minute, wait a minute! . . . on Hazel, your stenographer, it looks good, a platinum fox?
> Meyer, don't get me going like three eight day clocks! I must gotta have a platinum fox."
> "Okay," says Meyer, completely chastised, "so don't get excited, don't get exercised.
> And what do you want from that poor little Hazel? *Aza tayere shikse mit a karnose neyzl* [such a nice non-Jewish girl with a snub nose]. She works like a dog, without a vacation . . . "
> "Sits *nebekh* [stupidly] on your lap and takes your dictation. You think I don't know it, you think I'm an ox! So what's gonna be with that platinum fox?"[68]

Goldstein's songs are cleverly constructed satirical narratives of sexual innuendo. A generation later, some female performers (influenced undoubtedly by African American entertainers) would be much more direct. Belle Barth's ("My next story is a little risqué") records sold in the millions, and Pearl Williams rivaled Barth in popularity. Although both made use of Yiddish phrases in their routines, their performances were designed for late night club acts rather than vaudeville or cabaret.

Perhaps the most successful Yiddish "cross-over" comedian was the veteran vaudevillian Menashe Skulnik. Skulnik played the archetypal schlemiel. Indeed, familiarity with his persona

creates the humor of "Cordova, the Bronx Casanova," who boasts of his sexual attractiveness:

> I once spent a weekend in Turkey, showed the Sultan a thing or three,
> When I flew back, to my Bronx shack, the whole harem followed me.
> I'm Cordova, the Bronx Casanova, as a lover I'm known the world over,
> From Miami to Rome, I break up every home,
> I'm Cordova, the Bronx Casanova.[69]

In the 1950s, Skulnik found a suitable forum for his character in the new medium of television, making cameo appearances in sitcoms such as *The Goldbergs*, and briefly starring in his own variety show.[70] Of course many Yiddish comedians were unable or unwilling to cross over to English language comedy. Among the most endearing characters of Yiddish vaudeville was Getzel, a creation of the brilliant Yiddish monologuist Michel Rosenberg. Like his creator, Getzel is a man who cannot bridge the gap between the Old World and the New. He takes a train to the Bronx intending to hear a new cantor perform, follows the crowds to Yankee Stadium, and ends up believing that the players, with their white stockings, are a sect of Hasidim, and the umpire a Jewish choir master. A second trip to the Bronx finds him at a football game. When the quarterback screams out numbers, Getzel believes that he is at an auction, and starts calling out numbers of his own. But the funniest sketch has Getzel approached by a *landsmanshaft* burial society which banks on the idea that, by burying someone of Getzel's stature, it will attract people of a higher caliber. They offer the ailing Getzel a free plot on their cemetery (which has the advantage of being close to a subway and a cinema), a free burial, a burial shroud with two sets of pants, plus $18 a week while he is still alive. When Getzel shows signs of recovery, the society threatens to sue. A friend advises Getzel that it's best to avoid litigation, and that the simplest solution is—to die![71]

5.1. MOLLY PICON

The plays and films of Molly Picon, the darling of the Yiddish stage, presented humorous interpretations of the plight of first- and second-generation Jewish immigrants. Molly Picon's characters rebel against familial constraints and the restraints of traditional female roles, and according to one reviewer, audiences "recognize in her highly magnified or distorted humor the stuff which makes up their own lives."[72]

    Born in 1898, Picon made her first stage appearance at the age of 5, presenting a typical American

Molly Picon

vaudeville routine consisting of an English song, followed by a "Dutch" character recitation, and ending with a Russian dance.[73] Originally, she had set her ambitions on a Broadway career, and it was Jacob Kalich, her future husband and manager, who encouraged her to pursue a career in Yiddish theater. In 1911, when she was already a seasoned performer, Picon and Kalich embarked on a lengthy European engagement. The trip was designed to perfect her Yiddish, which she considered "completely bastardized," and to acquire the cachet of a European actress.[74]

Between 1911 and 1924, Picon gained experience in the Yiddish theaters of Vienna, Warsaw and Budapest. It was the play *Yankele,* written and produced by Kalich, and first performed in Vienna in 1921, that launched her to stardom. As Yankele, a *yeshiva bokher* (a male Talmud student), Picon found a signature that fitted both her talents and physique. Most of her subsequent successes—*East and West,* (1923), *The Little Devil* (1926), *The Circus Girl* (1928), *Yidl mit'n Fidl* (*Yidl with His Fiddle,*1936), and *Mamele* (1938)—would provide an opportunity to display her tomboy/flapper character, and engage in the cross-dressing routines which became the trademark of her long and successful career.

CROSSING BOUNDARIES

Performing Self, Performing Others

DIALECT HUMOR I

With the expansion of leisure time and disposable income in the later decades of the 19th century, vaudeville theater became increasingly popular. Reflecting the variety and stimulus of the urban environment (a typical vaudeville bill included dog shows, male, female and ethnic impersonations, magicians, mimics, and song and dance routines), the vaudeville stage introduced different groups of city-dwellers to the cultural intricacies of modern urban life.[75]

Shortly after the mass migration from Eastern Europe began in the 1880s, Jews established a substantial presence in this expanding industry, both as performers as well as managers. Like other vaudevillians, they, too, capitalized on humor as a vehicle for expressing the cultural incongruities which characterized the experience of their predominantly immigrant audiences, and which transcended the boundaries of ethnicity, class and neighborhood.

Dialect comedy was a vaudeville staple. In the wake of the mass migrations of the mid and late 19th century, older stock characters such as the blackface minstrel, or the "Yankee," were joined by "Irish," "Dutch" (i.e., German), "Italian," "Chinese" and eventually "Hebrew" comedians, in a sequence that roughly followed their order of arrival in America. The most famous "Dutch" comedians of the 1880s and 1890s was the team of Weber and Fields. Like many comedians of subsequent generations, Joe Weber and Lew Fields were the children of Jewish immigrants from Eastern Europe. Both grew up as East Side urchins, and picked up their acts by sneaking into neighborhood theaters. In 1879, at age twelve, they appeared as an Irish act, singing:

> "Here we are, an Irish pair
> Without any troubles or care
> We're here once more to make the people roar . . . "

As L. Marc Fields, great-great nephew of Lew Fields, notes

> With their Semitic profiles and dark eyes, they didn't
> look any more "Hibernian" than the blackface performer looked "Ethiopian." They turned this to their
> advantage: when they needed a big laugh right away,
> they'd enter singing "Here we are, an Irish pair," with

> their hands covering their noses. The gesture never
> failed to delight the Bowery audience.[76]

Eager to stand out in the competitive market of ethnic impersonators, they devised a "Dutch" act, in which their "German" accent was basically a bastardization of the Yiddish they spoke at home. In their stage relationship, Lew Fields would play Myer, the slick confidence man who usually triumphs over Mike (played by Joe Weber), the beleaguered plump and dumb man. Their acts had an aggressive, slapstick quality equally apparent in their dialogues:

> Mike: I am delightfulness to meet you.
> Myer: Der disgust is all mine.[77]

Weber and Fields became so popular that they opened their own music hall on Broadway in 1896, where, surrounded by a cast of star comedians and a glamorous female chorus line they staged elaborate burlesques of Broadway plays and current events, and satirized the pretensions of the upwardly mobile. Although they are scarcely remembered today, the influence of Weber and Fields on popular entertainment cannot be overestimated: These lavish revues inspired the Ziegfeld Follies, and a succeeding generation of theatrical innovators, including George and Ira Gershwin, Oscar Hammerstein II, Cole Porter, *Your Show of Shows* and *Saturday Night Live*. Their stage personas and team acts influenced Smith and Dale, Laurel and Hardy, Abbott and Costello, and Gleason and Carney.[78] Moreover, in their travesties, Weber and Fields elaborated a Jewish comic code which, in its transgressions and improprieties, presaged the humor of Fanny Brice, Eddie Cantor, and the Marx Brothers.

One of the first Jewish actors to specialize in Hebrew dialect comedy was David Warfield (*né* Wohlfelt). Warfield had his start as a member of the Weber and Fields team, where he performed Irish, German and Jewish character acts. Jewish impersonations, however, soon became his trademark. Appearing in a shabby, ill-fitting dark coat, his beard and hair unkempt, a pronounced nose, and a derby pulled over his head, his comedy routine depended heavily on a "Jewish" accent, mispronunciations and malapropisms. In a skit for a Weber and Fields revue entitled *Whirl-I-Gig*, he played "Sigmund Cohenski," a wealthy Jew vacationing in Paris, whose daughter fancies a dashing captain of the U.S. Navy. Upon hearing from his daughter that the captain is her idea of a hero, Cohenski replies:

"A hero! Is dot a business? A tailor is a business, a shoemaker is a business, but a hero? Better you should marry a bookkeeper."

"A bookkeeper? I suppose you think that the pen is mightier than the sword," the girl sneers.

"You bet my life," said Papa Cohenski. "Could you sign checks with a sword?"[79]

David Warfield in his "Hebrew" impersonation
(Museum of the City of New York)

Warfield's Cohenski illustrates the dilemma faced by Jewish "Hebrew" comedians. The first decade of the 20th century witnessed an unprecedented commercialization of comedy, stimulated by the increase both in leisure time as well as family budgets. This large scale exploitation of the joke was not limited to the vaudeville stage, but included the printing press and the early recording industry as well. Jewish comedians and entrepreneurs were particularly sensitive to the opportunities presented by this burgeoning market. The Jewish entrepreneur Henry Wehman, for instance, made a fortune with his compilations of ethnic humor, which also served as the basis for many dialect comedy routines.[80] Wehman even marketed dialect comedy outfits, such as "Hebrew" masks, to be used for home entertainment!

But the jokes compiled in his collections of "Hebrew" humor illustrate the winning formula in "Hebrew" comedy during this period:

Little Ike—"Fader, Mithter Isaacs wanth ter see yer."
Old Ike—"Tell him I'm out."

Hebrew Jokes and Dialect Humor. Witty Sayings and Rare Anecdotes. Original and Selected from our "Hebrew Friends." (Philadelphia: Royal Publishing Co, 1902) (Peter H. Schweitzer Collection)

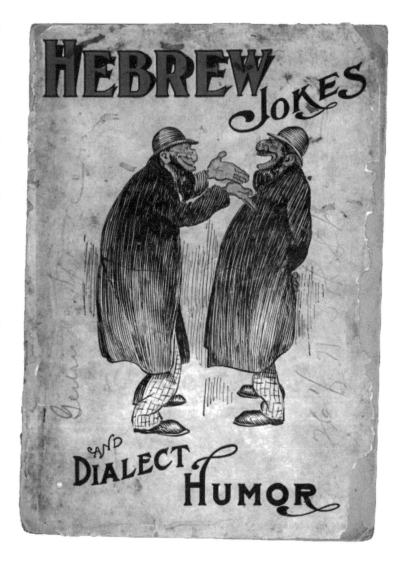

Little Ike—"Oh, fader, you told me you never told a lie!"

Old Ike—"Vell, I don't. You've got to go and tell it."[81]

Or the following:

"Solly, if your father promises a man twenty dollars a week, how many weeks will it take the man to get two hundred dollars?"

"Two hundred weeks," says Solly.

"Solly, you don't know your lesson."

"No," says Solly, "you don't know my fader."[82]

Many of these jokes confirmed the most negative Jewish stereotypes, particularly in regard to business ethics, cleanliness and sexuality. Indeed, the cover of Wehman's collection of *Hebrew Jokes*, showing a stereotypical Jew with Negroid features, suggests that the popularity of "Hebrew" humor did little to change the place of Jews within the racial taxonomy of early-twentieth-century America. Jewish comedy performances often came perilously close to reinforcing dominant anti-Semitic stereotypes. The distinction between audiences laughing with, or at Jews, was sufficiently blurry for some star comedians, such as Fanny Brice, to refuse to perform songs and routines that she felt to be anti-Jewish. Whatever she refused to perform, however, ended up in the repertoire of lesser Jewish stars.

Many "Hebrew" comedy routines exploited the rather benevolent and by now standard comic formula of the immigrant's cultural mistranslations, as in "Levinsky at the Wedding":

One thing I didn't like about Abe's wedding was right away it said at the top, "Your presents is requested." They can't wait to let you know you must help pay the expenses. And down at the bottom was "please come in evening dress." Ikey Blatt wore his pajamas.[83]

Most popular were the "Cohen on the Telephone" routines, which amplified the theme of cultural misunderstandings by introducing the new technology of the telephone. In one sketch, Cohen tries to speak to the bank manager, his landlord:

"Hullo! Hullo! Are you dere? Hullo! Vot number do I want? Vell, vot numbers have you got? Oh, excuse me, my mistook. I vant Central 248, please; yes, dot's right, 248. I say, miss, am I supposed to keep saying, 'Hullo!' and 'Are you dere?' until you come back again?"[84]

It was the English comedian Joe Hayman who first introduced Samuel Cohen as a phonograph character in Great Britain in 1912. Hayman subsequently published a volume of some twenty Cohen monologues together with a compilation of classic "Hebrew" jokes. Despite his claim of authorship, Hayman acknowledged that in humor, originality rarely applies, which was certainly the case for the iconic Jewish character Cohen. "You may have heard of the jokes before," Hayman writes in the book's preface, "but, as Mark Twain aptly put it, 'A *good* joke is *never* old.'"[85]

"Cohen on the Telephone" continued to be recorded throughout the 1920s and '30s by such comedians as Monroe

Silver, Barney Bernard, and George Sidney. The routine's popularity generated hundreds of thousands of record sales, with competing labels and performers issuing ever new versions of this instant classic. Monroe Silver was the most prolific, and his routines were issued on some two dozen labels and then transferred to radio in *Rudy Vallee's Fleischmann Hour*. As the collector Michael Corenthal writes in his catalog *Cohen on the Telephone*

> **When Cohen got tired of the telephone, there was the automobile, the houseboat, the opera, the sports arena and countless other comedic entanglements.**
>
> **The comic Jew in the form of the Cohen stories was quite an integrationist force. A Jewish personage became a permanent fixture in a majority of non-Jewish homes. The melting pot had finally melted something.[86]**

Well before the 1920s, the comic treatment of Jewish immigrants had lost its sharp edges. Instead of the stereotypical, lower-class ghetto Jew, Montague Glass's *Potash and Perlmutter* sketches (1910),

Barney Bernard and Alexander Carr as Potash and Perlmutter (1913) (New York Public Library for the Performing Arts at Lincoln Center)

featured two *allrightnik,* upwardly mobile Jewish clothing merchants, portrayed as lovable despite their sharp business sense. The 1913 stage adaptation, featuring Alexander Carr and Barney Bernard, became the longest running play of the year.

Highly popular with Jewish, as well as non-Jewish audiences in the 1910s and early '20s were songs with a "Yiddish" theme, such as "That's Yiddishe Love," "Yiddishe Rag," "Yiddishe Blues," "Yiddishe Charleston." A favorite in Jewish neighborhoods was the song "Nat'an, Nat'an, Tell Me For What Are You Waitin'."

> Nat'an and Rosalie, they both kept company,
> They both kept company for six long years.
> And every time she'd ask him, "When will you marry me?"
> He said, "I don't make enough salary."
> Each time Nat'an tried to kiss her Rosalie cried.
> "Nat'an, Nat'an. Tell me for what are you waitin', Nat'an?"

As Irving Berlin, composer of many "Yiddishe" melodies conceded many years later, the comic twist

Sheet music: "Nat'an, Nat'an!, Tell Me For What Are You Waitin'?" (1916) (Spertus Museum)

Sheet music: "Abie's Irish Rose" (1923) (Spertus Museum)

of these songs "would no longer be taken in the spirit in which they had been written" by subsequent genera-tions.[87] But even at the time, the stereotypical portrayal of Jews in dialect comedy did encounter strong reactions from Jewish organizations such as B'nai B'rith, as well as from other established middle-class Jews. At the basis of the controversy over "Hebrew humor" was the charge that in their appeal to a broad audience, Jewish comedians were exposing the foibles of their kin.

One of the most vocal groups campaigning for the abo-lition of what it saw as the "buffoonery of the Jew" was the Chicago Anti Stage-Jew Ridicule Committee, headed by Miss Mollie Eda Osherman. In a circular letter of Sep-tember 1913, which received widespread press coverage, the group called on Chicago Jews to be vigilant:

> If, inadvertently, you should attend a playhouse
> where the Jew is the target of the comedian's vul-
> gar horse-play for the gusto of the audience, regis-
> ter at once a vigorous protest to the management.
> The Jew has submitted long enough to public slurs
> and insults on the stage.

In a public response to the call, one letter writer point-ed to the paradox of such an initiative, observing that "such distortions . . . appeal less to a genteel audience than to members of the race themselves . . . Moreover, nearly all the Jew impersonators are Hebrews themselves, and they get their engagements in most cases from Hebrew managers."[88]

Eager not to alienate ethnic audiences (the Irish engaged in similar protests), major vaudeville circuits, such as Keith and Albee, responded to these objections by instituting a policy of self-censorship. As a result, performers became extremely sensitive to the need to win public approval for their acts. Willie and Eugene Howard even gave out press reports claiming that "every gag we have ever used we have submitted to a rabbi who is a friend of ours and who must approve it before we use it."[89]

In the 1920s and '30s, the focus of Jewish comedy shifted to exploiting the comic possibilities inherent in the growing intimacy between Jews and other ethnic groups. Inter-ethnic courting rituals, romances and marriage provided a favorite comic theme. The archetypal comic/romantic plot was provided by the Irish-Jewish liaison. Film comedies such as *Abie's Irish Rose* (1928); *Private Izzy Murphy* (1926); *Sailor Izzie Murphy* (1927); *Clancy's Kosher Wedding* (1927); *Kosher Kitty Kelly* (1926), and the highly popular *Cohens and Kellys* series (1926)—which starred the veteran Jewish comedian George Sidney[90]—used the Irish/Jewish romance to dramatize a ritual of assimilation. In part, the films' humor rested on the contrast between the comic and grotesque first-generation Jew and Irish with their handsome and "respectable" Americanized offspring. The incongruity of different ethnic customs, brought together through marriage, provided another source of laughter, as the lyrics to the song "Abie's Irish Rose" illustrate:

And to show his folks how nice I am
On Friday night I don't eat ham
Which absolutely shows I'm Abie's Irish Rose
My best friend Maggie Finnegan
Will be right by my side
His best friend Jake will cut the cake
When I become a bride
We'll all march out and in again
The like you've never seen
We'll dance to "Eli, Eli" and "Wearin' of the Green"
Everybody knows I'm Abie's Irish Rose,
The things he eats I'll have to eat them, too
Tho' it's against my wish I'll make gefilte fish
And now and then I'll sneak a look
In Mrs. Ginsburg's cooking book[91]

DIALECT HUMOR II

By the early 20th century, entrepreneurs, such as the Shubert brothers, Marcus Loew and Adolph Zukor (later to become major Hollywood moguls) transformed vaudeville by rationalizing the booking system and setting up circuits which contracted strings of theaters across the country to book the same bill.[92] The booming industry propelled numerous Jewish comedians to national stardom: Sophie Tucker, Al Jolson, George Jessel, Eddie Cantor, Fanny Brice, Jack Benny, George Burns, George Sidney, Milton Berle, Belle Baker, Ted Lewis, Bennie

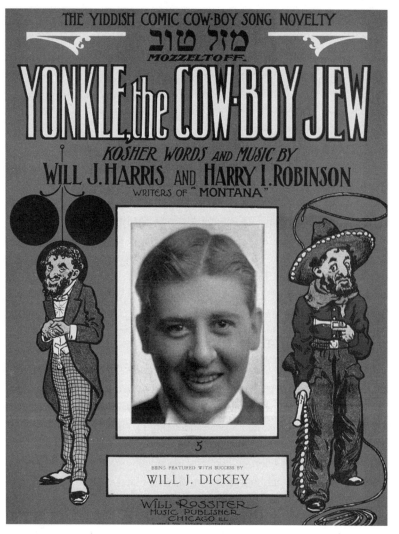

Fields, Smith and Dale, the Howard Brothers, and the Marx Brothers are only some of the Jewish names that came to dominate stage and screen.

The prominence of Jewish entertainers in early 20th-century American culture speaks to the ambition and persistence of these children of immigrants. A career in vaudeville required little or no entry capital or education, and provided an opportunity to contribute to meager family incomes. Many budding performers developed their talents by imitating the wide variety of accents, dialects and gestures they encountered on the streets of the ghetto. Sneaking into neighborhood vaudeville theaters, they picked up "Dutch" routines, "Irish" impersonations, blackface acts, "Hebrew" comedy, sentimental ballads and slapstick, which they then performed on amateur nights.

Versatility was the key to success. Facing fierce competition, and attempting to show off their virtuosity, ethnic impersonators first devised character-change acts, in which they would switch effortlessly among various ethnic roles. For example, Frank Bush, in a single act would appear as a Jew, a German, and a Yankee farmer. A similar eclecticism is apparent in

Sheet music: "Yonkle, The Cow-boy Jew" (1907)
(Peter H. Schweitzer Collection)

the career of the Lower East Side Jewish songwriter Irving Berlin. In addition to "Yiddishe" pastiche, compositions with a Jewish motif such as "Yiddishe Eyes," "Yiddle on Your Fiddle, Play Some Ragtime," "Good-Bye Becky Cohen," and "Sadie Salome, Go Home," (popularized by Fanny Brice in 1909), Berlin wrote "Irish" pastiche ("I wish that you was my Gal, Molly"), Italian pastiche ("Dorando"), German dialect songs with such titles as "Oh! How That German Could Love," and "Colored Romeo," a mock version of what was then commonly referred to as a "coon" song, as well.[93]

The adoption of African American musical styles by Jewish Tin Pan Alley composers such as Irving Berlin and George Gershwin has been well documented. But the connection between "Hebrew" impersonation and blackface performance was equally striking. Blackface minstrelsy, the favorite form of popular entertainment for most of the 19th century, in the early 20th century had been absorbed by vaudeville as one form of dialect comedy. By 1910, it had become an almost exclusively Jewish domain. Jewish vaudeville entertainers such as George Burns, Eddie Cantor, George Jessel and Al Jolson were as likely to be performing

Sheet music: "Sadie Salome, Go Home!" (1909)
(Peter H. Schweitzer Collection)

"Hebrew types" as to be donning blackface. Indeed, before Al Jolson became famous in *The Jazz Singer* as a Jewish son who abandons his career as a cantor for the lure of the American stage as a blackface performer, in vaudeville Jolson alternated between "Hebrew" acts such as "The Hebrew and his Cadet" (in which he teamed up with brother Harry) and comic "coon" songs such as "Where Did Robinson Crusoe Go with Friday on Saturday Night," which he performed in blackface.

The meaning of this donning of blackface—however condemned by contemporary standards—should be interpreted in the context of a performance tradition which banked on ethnic caricature and to which realism or authenticity of representation were foreign concepts. Moreover, according to Ronald Sanders, the Jewish use of blackface must be seen in light of the Jews' fondness for ethnic pastiche. Rather than mindlessly adopting the African American stereotypes conjured up by minstrelsy, for Jewish entertainers the use of blackface was an act of identification. In the plight of African Americans, Jews found a mirror to their own history of exclusion and suffering. Blackface, according to Irving Howe, came to serve as "a mask for Jewish expressiveness, with one woe speaking through the voice of another."[94]

A perfect example of how self-conscious ethnic pastiche could be is provided by the "Yiddishe" song "Yiddle on Your Fiddle, Play Some Rag Time," written in 1909 by Irving Berlin. The song is about a Jewish wedding, described in music and words, in which Yiddle, the fiddler, starts playing ragtime, and is egged on by Sadie with the chorus containing the title phrase. The music shifts to suggest the conventions of ragtime, to which Sadie responds by calling the fiddler "mine choc'late baby."

The humor of the song, as Sanders suggests, plays on Jews acting black![95] But at the same time, the joke is about Jews acting "Jewish." As Jewish performers transformed blackface into a vehicle for self-expression, they broke out of the constraints of the older "Hebrew" comic and began using Jewish dialect humor to counter stereotypes and interpret Jewish culture to Jewish as well as non-Jewish audiences.

Sophie Tucker inserted Yiddishisms into her Red Hot Mama melodies "just to give the audience a kick," and topped off her performances with renditions of "Eli, Eli." Fanny Brice, in lavish French aristocratic dress and waving her fan, impersonated Madame du Barry, the mistress of Louis XV, and declaimed in an unmistakably Yiddish accent: "I may be a bad voman, but demm good company."

One generation removed from the immigrant experience, many of these comedians made Jewish life, culture and language the focus of their humor. Al Jolson and Eddie Cantor imitated their cantor fathers; and George Jessel created a tradition when he telephoned his Jewish mother on stage:[96]

"Hello, Mama, this is Georgie from the checks every week . . . So how do you like the bird I gave you? . . . You cooked it? Mama, that was a very valuable bird. It spoke five languages . . . .He should have said something?"[97]

Smith and Dale's Dr. Kronkhite made use of exaggerated Jewish inflections and gestures:

Patient: "What do I owe you?"

Doctor: "You owe me $10 for my advice."

Patient: "$10 for your advice? Well, Doctor, here is $2. Take it, that's my advice."

Doctor: "You cheapskate! You shnorrer, you low life, you racoon, you baboon!"

Patient: "One more word from you, you'll only get $1."

Doctor: "You . . . "

Patient: "That's the word! Here's a dollar."[98]

Jewish dialect humor also appeared in print. It infused Harry Hershfield's cartoon strip "Abie the Agent," which featured a Jewish businessman/detective and ran for years as a syndicated cartoon in American newspapers. Milt Gross's *Nize Baby* (1925) presented Jewish interpretations of popular fairy tales:

"Nize baby!!! Itt opp all de wheatinna—so momma' gonna tell you from "Leedle Rad Ridink Hoot!"[99]

6.1 FANNY BRICE

Reflecting on her success as a performer, Fanny Brice commented:

Fate and my Jewish blood have been kind to me. I believe it's because I'm Jewish that I have been a steady climber on the stage. Not that my success has been brought by my imitations of Jewish types, but the versatility with which I have been credited, is peculiar to the Jews. There is no need of my giving historical justification for my statement, as scholars have long determined that a variety of experiences, and a constantly changing environment have produced an adaptability in the Jew, rarely possessed by other people.[100]

Fanny Borach, as she was called before she adopted the stage name Brice, first developed her own mimic talents through her familiarity with the Polish, Hungarian and German of the immigrant servant girls employed by her middle-class mother. In 1909, she got her first break in a burlesque show, where she performed "Sadie Salome," an Irving Berlin song about a Jewish girl who leaves home for the stage and is implored by her boyfriend Mose:

When his Sadie came to sight,
He stood up and yelled with all his might
Don't do that dance, I tell you Sadie,
That's not a bus'ness for a lady!
Most e'rybody knows
That I'm your loving Mose
Oy oy oy—where's your clothes?[101]

Heeding Irving Berlin's advice, she performed the song with an exaggerated Jewish accent. It was an instant hit, and brought her to the attention of Florenz Ziegfeld, who engaged her for his Ziegfeld Follies, which had recently become one of Broadway's main attractions.[102] Performances of Jewish songs

FANNIE BRICE'S SECRET OF HOW TO KEEP SMILING

Radio Stars

THE LARGEST CIRCULATION OF ANY RADIO MAGAZINE

JUNE
10
CENTS

THE
CANDID PICTURE
MAGAZINE
OF RADIO

COMPLETE
COAST-TO-COAST
PROGRAM LISTINGS

FANNIE
BRICE

Courtesy of William Brice

became Brice's trademark. In her interpretations, she adopted the persona of a "spunky, poor Jewish girl longing for love and fame," imbuing the lyrics with

> the spirit of Loscha of the Coney Island popcorn counter and Marta of the cheeses at Brodsky's delicatessen, and the Sadies and Rachels and the Birdies with the turnover heels at the Second Avenue dance halls.[103]
> Many have suggested that my best audiences must be the very Jewish ones . . . But the contrary is true. To the very East-Side Jew, who sees me gesturing with my hands, shrug my shoulders, and murder the English language, it seems a natural, almost commendable thing. How then can he laugh at himself? . . . It is the Gentile, to whom these gestures are alien, who is himself very placid in his speech, who sees the humor in my exaggerations . . . . My best audiences, however, are composed of "American Jews"—who combine, in a certain sense, the Jew and the Gentile. They have seen the awkward gesticulation; they have heard the comic speech, at close range, but they have passed beyond that stage, and so it is they who see the ludicrousness of Fanny Brice, it

Fanny Brice as Baby Snooks
(Wisconsin Center for Theater and Film Research)

is they who appreciate her imitations, it is they who laugh at her exaggerations.[104]

At the same time, Brice sought to avoid the degrading elements of earlier vaudeville "Hebrew" characterizations.

I never did a routine that would offend my race because I depended on my race for the laughs. In anything Jewish I ever did, I wasn't standing apart making fun. I was the race and what happened to me on the stage is what could happen to my people. They identified with me, which made it all right to get a laugh. Because they were laughing at me as much as they were laughing at themselves.[105]

Brice used Yiddish for comic effect: her humor rested on the incongruity of the "Indian squaw" Rosie Rosenstein, or her heavily made up seductive women (the silent screen vamp Theda Bara, or the royal *maitresses* Mme Pompadour or Mme Du Barry) speaking with the "vocal inflections of the Lower East Side."[106] She mocked the pretensions of ballet dancers (pronounced "belly densehs"), the self-involvement of famous contemporary silent screen vamps or the excesses of celebrated women of literature and history. Sometimes, her routines displayed a pronounced political consciousness: in a 1924 revue, the year in which Congress passed stringent immigration restrictions, she sang Irving Berlin's song "Don't Send Me Back to Petrograd." Appearing as a despondent, forlorn immigrant, with only a few belongings and clothed in a shawl and a torn dress,

she begs immigration officials to let her stay in the United States, singing, in a sarcastic comment on the xenophobia that was overtaking America: "I promise to work the best I can, I'll even wash the sheets of the Ku Klux Klan."[107]

Brice also was an impressive melodramatic actress and singer, who became famous for her rendition of the song "My Man." In the late 1920s, when the "talkie" created a revolution in the film industry, Brice, like many other vaudeville performers, tried her luck in Hollywood. But her film career soon floundered. With films reaching the American heartland, stars were under pressure to adjust their speech and image for mainstream rather than East Coast audiences. According to *Variety*, her persona was simply too Jewish.[108] But for her colleague and friend Molly Picon, Brice's lack of screen success was a result of her own desire to normalize her stage persona. According to Picon, after she had her nose "fixed," Fanny "just wasn't funny anymore."[109] Eventually, Brice transformed her rather awkward Jewish persona into a character adapted to mainstream audiences. As Baby Snooks, the primary character of her successful radio show, she became a fixture of American family life in the late 1930s and '40s.

6.2. EDDIE CANTOR

The career of Eddie Cantor exemplifies the same sensitivity to roles, gestures and speech as many other Jewish performers who were his contemporaries. To a significant extent, this sensitivity was home-bred. Describing his grandmother who raised

Eddie Cantor in the film *Whoopee!* (1930) (Wisconsin Center for Film and Theater Research)

(inset)
Eddie Cantor in the film *Palmy Days* (1931) (Wisconsin Center for Film and Theater Reseach)

Courtesy of Brian Gari

Courtesy of Brian Gari

him, Eddie Cantor relates that she spoke "in Yiddish, Polish, Russian, or a mixture of the three." For these children of immigrants, languages and cultures existed not as separate entities, but as intersected and superimposed in fluid and often absurd ways. Perhaps more than any other performer, Eddie Cantor transformed those early experiences into a strikingly transgressive performance style.

Cantor's predeliction for cultural pastiche was already evident early in his career when many of his routines were done in blackface. He would, for example, play "Salome" in blackface, "combining racial impersonation with a veiled transvestite burlesque."[110] After his 1917 debut in the Ziegfeld Follies, Cantor developed a vaudeville persona that emphasized his Jewishness. His "Moe the Tailor" sketch for the 1929 Follies, with its parody of Jewish mannerisms, appealed both to Jews as well as to middle-class audiences fascinated by the exoticism of the ghetto.

In an effort to profit from the interest in Jewish actors among East Coast audiences, as well cash in on the American fascination with the Jew as Other, in the early 1930s, two Ziegfeld Revues which starred Eddie Cantor were adapted for the screen. In *Glorifying the American Girl* (1929), a movie that explored the world of New York show business, Cantor's speech is heavily inflected with Yiddishisms and cantorial intonations. *Whoopee* (1930) foregrounded Eddie Cantor's Jewishness even more explicitly. The pressbook advertisement promised "laughs, giggles and roars . . . when Cantor starts to cut up as a Jewish Indian."[111]

The plot of the movie revolves around the thwarted romance between a male Indian (who later turns out to be "white" and adopted at birth by an Indian chief) and a female WASP. Cantor assumes a series of disguises—hypochondriac, black cook, cowboy-outlaw, Indian and Jew—(the latter a reenactment of his Moe the Tailor character). In the most burlesque scene, Cantor, masquerading as an Indian, tries to sell an Indian blanket and doll, and gradually shifts from exagger-

ated Indian speech to the accent and gestures of a Lower East Side peddler:

> "Look, if I sell you for $40, I couldn't make a cent. I should live—it costs me alone thirty-five and a half dollars—so I should sell you for $40? Such a *chutzpah*! *Ir darf zikh shemen*! [You should be ashamed of yourself!]"

Cantor's routine calls attention to the strict racial categories that drive the plot of the movie, and constitutes the subversive element of this use of cultural pastiche. While failing to meet contemporary standards of political correctness, pastiche sends a powerful message about the constructed nature of race, indeed of all cultural categories, suggesting, too, why humor has an insidious ability to turn the world as we know it upside down.

While both films were hits in New York, they failed to attract audiences in the American heartland. This failure led to the remaking of Cantor's image. The advertising campaign for his next film, *Palmy Days*, (1930) promoted Cantor as an all-American boy. Press photographs displayed Cantor eating Wonder Bread, while Cantor's song in the movie, "Dunk, dunk, dunk," inspired a donut dunking campaign.[112]

This whitewashing of Cantor's image was part of a larger trend in the American culture industry during the late 1930s, and would later earn him opprobrium in Lenny Bruce's "What's Jewish/What's Goyish" monologue. For Bruce, Cantor, not surprisingly, was as goyish as Wonder Bread!

6.3. THE MARX BROTHERS

If the cultural critic Gilbert Seldes deemed "daemonic" the appropriate term for characterizing the performances of Fanny Brice, what term would he have reserved for the Marx Broth-

ers, who carried this subversion of language, cultural decorum and social hierarchies to the brink? While their genius for simple mimicry is evident in such films as *Monkey Business* (Groucho appears in successive impersonations of a "patriotic stump speaker, dance instructor, quiz show host, little boy and

Still from *A Night at the Opera*
(Wisconsin Center for Film and
Theater Research)

flitatious woman"),[113] the comedy of the Marx Brothers, first and foremost, is a comedy of "verbal assault."[114] This sensitivity to the spoken word, reflected in Chico's pseudo-Italian dialect and seemingly mindless banter, Groucho's verbal acrobatics, and even in Harpo's silence, is not surprising consider-

ing the fact that language was the cornerstone of the family's survival. According to Harpo, the boys' father, Frenchie Marx,

**was born in a part of Alsace-Lorraine that had
stayed loyal to Germany, even when France ruled the**

Lobby Card for *A Night at the Opera* (Academy of Motion Pictures Arts and Sciences)

province. So while the official language was French, at home the Marxes spoke "Plattdeutsch," low-country German. When the family came to America, they naturally gravitated toward immigrants who spoke the same dialect. On the upper East Side of Manhattan . . . a sort of Plattdeutsch Society sprang up—unofficial, but tightly knit. Anybody who spoke Plattdeutsch was okay with Frenchie, had his undying trust. And since Frenchie was one of the few tailors in the city who spoke Plattdeutsch he got a lot of business out of sheer sentiment, that he never deserved. If it weren't for the mutual loyalty of Frenchie and his *landsmen*, the Marx brothers wouldn't have stayed under the same roof long enough to have become acquainted, let alone go forth in show business.[115]

In the Marx Brothers' comedies, words are made strange, and their meanings utterly corrupted. The nonsense dialogues between Chico and Harpo had its comical foundation in the incommensurability of immigrant dialect and standard English. The "viaduct" ("Why a Duck") routine from *Cocoanuts* is a classic example. But in terms of sheer absurdity, this dialogue from *Animal Crackers* is unequalled. After Chico hypothesizes that a missing painting was devoured by left-handed moths, Groucho's character, Captain Spaulding, requests that Chico leave, and then says,

"I'd buy you a parachute if I thought it wouldn't open." But Chico immediately disables the viciousness of

Groucho's remark with another pun: "I got a pair of shoes [parachute]."

The punning continues when it is suggested that they go to court to request the return of the missing painting. When Chico seems mystified by this, Groucho asks, "Didn't you ever see a Habeas Corpus?"

To which Chico responds, "No, but I see *habeas* Irish Rose" punning on the popular movie *Abie's Irish Rose*.[116]

As various scholars have noted, this subversion of normality also carries over into the realm of class and status differentiations. The plots of Marx Brothers' movies typically revolve around immigrant schemes to make fast money and gain entry into the exclusive worlds of class and culture. By merely adopting upper-class roles and assuming the status that comes with them, the immigrant (momentarily) gains the upper hand. Groucho's ill-fitting tails and cigars, which mimic the signs of the social elite, are mistaken for the "real" by high society, symbolized by the Margaret Dumont character. Chico's virtuoso trick piano playing and his brother's dexterity at the harp (especially evident in *A Night at the Opera*) sabotage the exclusivity of high culture—a subversive strategy that reappears in the performances of numerous other Jewish comedians.

Even if their successes as scam artists are usually short-lived, their skewed perspective infects the world around them. In that sense, the Marx Brothers' comic strategy goes well beyond travesty. Through radical decentering, they continually impose their own logic upon society, making what is marginal—the immigrant—central.

6.4 THE ERASURE OF JEWISHNESS

By the 1930s, American film studios had changed from privately owned firms to large corporations, marketing products for national, rather than regional audiences. Jewish comedy stars were forced to downplay their Jewishness. At the same time, even more vociferously than before, Jewish groups demanded the removal of damaging stereotypes from stage and screen. In response to such campaigns, the projected title for a George Jessel movie, *Schlemiel* (1927) was changed to *Mamma's Boy*.[117]

The 1934 Hays code, designed to protect religious groups against ridicule, dealt a further blow to the stage tradition of the comic Jew. And the rise of anti-Semitism completed the erasure of Jewishness from American popular culture. Hollywood moguls were determined to avoid provoking any suspicion of Hollywood as dominated by Jews and Jewish interests, and they discouraged the production of films with overtly Jewish themes.

By 1935, most of the conspicuously Jewish comedians had disappeared from the screen. Veteran actors such as George Sidney (the star of *The Cohens and Kellys*) were unable to find work; and the dialect comedian Lou Holtz was forced off the air after listeners complained he was anti-Semitic.[118] Stars who looked "too Jewish" were either made over to look more mainstream or banished from the screen altogether; movie scripts were purged of traces of Jewish life; and characters originally scripted as Jews reemerged in film versions as white-bread Americans, or Irishmen!

In an ambivalent tribute to the vaudeville tradition of ethnic impersonation, Charlie Chaplin, in his movie *The Great Dictator* (1940) assumes the double role of a Jewish ghetto barber and dictator Adenoid Hynkel of Tomania, a parody of Hitler. Despite the film's importance as an early Hollywood attempt to address the plight of European Jewry, the movie stands as a testament to the erasure of Jewishness: in *The Great Dictator*, Jews are represented as an underclass, without any markers to signify a unique culture other than suffering and enclosure inside the ghetto.

This Jewish disappearance is evident, too, in the career of Danny Kaye. After his first screen test at Metro-Goldwyn-Mayer, Samuel Goldwyn recognized Kaye's talent but insisted that his nose was too large. Kaye refused to have it "fixed" but did agree to a compromise: he bleached his hair.[119] Since then, his clownish persona remained devoid of any allusions to his ethnic background. He did, however, capitalize on the schlemiel persona and parodies of foreign languages, acts he developed during his years as a Catskills entertainer. Kaye's humor marked a trend in Jewish humor which was to predominate during the 1940s and '50s, a period characterized by what the critic Henry Popkin described as the "de-Semitization" of American culture.[120]

Writers and comedians continued to perform comic codes of Jewishness—codes that go back to the early days of immigration. But Jewish humor became a secret language, a silent wink to fellow Jews, communicated through personae, gestures, and allusions in speech which went largely unnoticed by the non-Jewish public. As bold pronouncements of this linger-

ing, underground Jewish presence on the screen, Yiddish phrases and Jewish inflections would occasionally prop up in the performances of Eddie Cantor, Groucho Marx, Danny Kaye, the cartoon character Betty Boop, and in the late 1950s and early 1960s in the film comedies of Billy Wilder (most notably *Some Like it Hot* and *The Apartment*).

With the disappearance of the comic Jew, Jews lost their single most important public venue for self-representation, and they increasingly appeared in the popular media solely in the guise of victims. This irony was perceived by some even as it occurred. In 1944 , the Hollywood producer Ben Hecht noted:

> **He is safe now, the little Jew. No baggy pants, no oversized derby jammed over his ears, no mispronunciations or waving of hands. The caricature has been wiped out.**
>
> **With it has gone the open-heartedness, the quick sentimentality, the eagerness for fun; most of all this genius for fun—the half-mad capering of irony and jest that is the oldest of all the Jewish tradition . . . . And with the vanishing of the caricature, the original himself has become invisible . . . A generation has**

Danny Kaye
(Wisconsin Center for Film and Theater Research)

grown up without having seen or heard of a Jew—except as a massacre victim or a world menace. No greater kidnapping has ever been witnessed.[121]

Perhaps most poignantly, the tenuous status of the comic Jew in post-World War II America is evident in the career of Sam Levenson, who started as a dialect comedian. One favorite routine, "Basic Yiddish Lessons," consisted of a parodic Berlitz-like course in Yiddish terms and expressions. In the 1950s, however, Levenson vehemently disavowed the self-denigrating aspects of what he termed stories about the "Little Jew," including his own dialect humor. Responding to Henry Popkin's lament about the "de-Semitization" of American culture, Levinson wrote,

> Mr. Popkin feels that by rejecting dialect we are "sha-sha-ing," Aryanizing, that we are dishonestly eliminating a section of Jewish humor that should be given free play . . . . I admit that in my own work I have deliberately expurgated dialect stories. I'll tell you why, too. I was in the audience of a night club while a famous "dialectician" was regaling a predominantly Gentile audience with stories of shrewd businessmen, of fat and uncultured Jewish women in mink coats, stories of how Jews outwit Gentiles—and the audience howled. The laughter frightened me. The entire scene recalled the Nazi beer hall where comedians with derby hats and beards told the same type of story to those who were later to become the executioners of our people. This may sound extreme, but it is my belief that any Jew who, in humor or otherwise, strengthens the misconceptions and the prejudices against his own people is neither a good Jew nor a responsible human being. There are such things as "inside jokes," . . . which a people tolerates within its own ranks. These inside-isms are very common in Yiddish parlance, yet I would not use them in English before a Gentile audience . . .[122]

RADIO

Jewish Humor as American Family Ritual

With the onset of the Great Depression, attendance at vaudeville theaters dropped dramatically, and theaters either closed their doors or curtailed their performances. Out on the streets or facing heavy financial cutbacks, many vaudevillians looked for employment elsewhere, and found it in the new medium of radio. Unlike theater, radio was relatively inexpensive to produce, and, with radio sets sold on installment, it provided millions of listeners with a cheap form of entertainment.

As Lizabeth Cohen argues, early radio broadcasting had a distinctly grassroots orientation. Technological limitations, most importantly the limited broadcasting range, initially ensured that radio stations were mostly sponsored by local institutions such as ethnic, religious and labor groups which used the medium as a form of promotion. Jewish radio stations, for example, featured programs devoted to Yiddish vaudeville. Competing for audiences, commercial radio networks programmed so-called nationality hours, and recruited performers such as Molly Picon to star in their own programs.[123] By the late 1920s, network stations had all but driven out the grassroots stations, and by the late 1930s, they developed a format that came to be known as situation comedy, featuring weekly broadcasts of well-known comedians such as Ed Wynn, Milton Berle, George Burns and Gracie Allen, surrounded by a supporting cast.

7.1: THE GOLDBERGS

One of the most successful new radio shows was *The Goldbergs*, written by, and starring Gertrude Berg. The daughter of a Catskills resort owner, Gertrude Berg had taken to writing and performing skits in order to entertain the guests at her parents' hotel. Looking for a way to replenish her own family's resources, depleted by the Depression, Berg approached CBS with a pilot for a show, inspired by Milt Gross's dialect stories, which were then being broadcast. Berg herself was asked to read the script, which she had deliberately delivered in illegible handwriting, and was immediately cast in the role of Molly Goldberg.

The radio broadcast of *The Goldbergs* ran almost continuously from 1929 until 1950. It attracted millions of listeners, and rated second only to the *Amos 'n Andy Show* in popularity. In 1949 the show premiered on television, where it ranked between Milton Berle and Arthur Godfrey in the top three rat-

ings. A screen version, entitled *The Rise of the Goldbergs*, was distributed in 1951. Over the years, Americans came to consider the Goldbergs as an extension of their own families. Indeed, when another actress filled in for Berg, temporarily unable to play because of a sore throat, 30,000 fans wrote letters of protest. One year, a group of nuns asked Berg for copies of the scripts they had missed when they gave the show up for Lent![124]

In part, the secret to the show's popularity lay in its combination of realism and dialect humor. While avoiding the crudeness of old-style dialect comedy, *The Goldbergs* exploited the language and foibles of its main characters. In the earlier episodes, the dialogue was characterized by its Yiddish inflection. Molly would say to her son:

"Vat's de matter so late, Sammy? Let me look on your hends. Playing marbles, ha? For vat is your fadder slaving for vat I'm esking you? A marble shooter you'll gonna be? A beautiful business for a Jewish boy!"[125]

As the Goldbergs became more established, their language changed. The dialogue now focussed on Gertrude's malapropisms (known as Mollyisms or Goldbergisms). Molly would say things like: "It's late, Jake, and time to expire."[126] Or, "I'm putting on my bathrobe and condescending the stairs."[127] On the tongue of Jews, English could also be a funny language. The financial situation of the Goldberg family also changed over time. The husband, Jake, a tailor who lost his savings in the Depression, became a manufacturer and earned enough to move the family from the Lower East Side to the Bronx—a move made by countless other Jewish families.

But the key to the success of *The Goldbergs* was its strategy of dual address. The show appealed as much to Jews, who could relish the public representation of their culture, as to non-Jews. Although they might sound different, fundamentally the Goldbergs were just like millions of other American families, struggling through the Depression and war, and aspiring to achieve middle-class status. "There are surface differences," according to Berg, "but these surface differences only serve to emphasize how much alike most people are."[128]

Although *The Goldbergs* promoted inter-cultural understanding, the show deliberately steered away from controversial subjects such as politics, racism, anti-Semitism, zionism and unionism. As in another popular contemporary show about an immigrant family, *I Remember Mama*, ethnicity was safely conflated with domesticity and encapsulated within the universal icon of the matriarch. Indeed, in 1950 Molly Goldberg was honored by the Girls Club of America as the Radio and TV Mother of the Year. That same year, she was also awarded an Emmy for Best Actress in a continuing performance.

The Goldbergs ran into trouble in the early 1950s when its male lead, Philip Loeb, was blacklisted for alleged Communist ties. Forced to fire him by the show's financial underwriters, Berg kept him on salary as long as she could. (Unable to find work, Loeb would commit suicide in 1955.) A combination of steadily declining ratings and lack of sponsorship kept the show off the air for eight months, and finally culminated in its cancellation in 1955. Assessing the demise of what had once been America's favorite radio and television family, one critic concluded that Molly Goldberg's "language, cute as it always is . . . is contrived to meet outmoded expectations. For one thing, television audiences today do not find the portrait of a domineering, sheltering matriarch exactly comfortable."[129]

Or could it also be that by the middle '50s, in their search for social mobility and acceptance, Jewish audiences, too, had begun to feel the constraint of the Jewish family? Indeed, within a decade, Dan Greenburg's volume *How To Be A Jewish Mother*, with its comic representation of the smothering Jewish mother, would hit the best-seller list, spinning off a Broadway adaptation starring Molly Picon, and an audio recording featuring none other than Gertrude Berg herself.

7.2: JACK BENNY

During the 1930s and '40s, *The Jack Benny Show* rivaled *The Goldbergs* in popularity. While Molly Goldberg strove to represent the archetypal matriarch, the appeal of Jack Benny was based on his "Everyman" personality.[130] Yet, the two shows represented opposite directions in American popular entertainment. Neither in his acts nor in his style of delivery did Jack Benny ever identify himself explicitly as a Jew. He made no apparent use of Yiddish, or Jewish dialect. Although outwardly, Jack Benny did not display a specific link to the immigrant experience, he was born Benjamin Kubelsky in Waukegan, Illinois on Feb. 14, 1894. His immigrant father,

Meyer Kubelsky, was in the garment business. In his early teens, Benny joined the vaudeville circuit as a pit musician, and soon found an audience for funny routines on his violin. By 1926, he made it to Broadway. His major breakthrough, however, came when he plunged into the new medium of radio. Relatively unknown when he started on NBC in 1932, within two years *The Jack Benny Show* was a hit, and by 1940 Benny was radio's number one personality. During the Depression and afterwards, his Sunday afternoon broadcasts became an American family ritual.[131]

With uncanny intuition, in radio, and after 1950, on television, Benny cultivated a familial intimacy. The show was a cross between variety, with its emphasis on gags and music, and sitcom. But the humor of *The Jack Benny Show* derived from its star's relationships with his African American valet Rochester (played by Eddie Anderson), and Mary Livingston, his occasional girlfriend (played by Benny's wife, *née* Sadie Marks, a relative of the Marx Brothers).

Like Kaye's persona, Benny's character contained coded references to his Jewishness, particularly in his own schlemiel character and his proverbial stinginess. In what is perhaps his most famous routine, an armed gangster accosts Benny and threatens: "Your money or your life!" Benny remains silent, for six or seven seconds. The hoodlum becomes impatient and repeats the question. In a thin, wailing voice pleading for time, Benny responds: "I'm thinking it over!"[132] Other attrib-

utes of Benny's character habitually exploited for gags were his eternal bachelorhood, his effeminacy, particularly in contrast to more masculine cameos, his sensitivity about age, his cowardliness, envy, and mean-spiritedness. At the same time, Benny's favorite self-demeaning question was "Did you ever see such a jerk?"[133] His key prop was the violin, which served mostly as a set-up for sensitivity about musical talent.

Benny did use Jewish characters as comic foils. Although his early sidekick, Mr. Schlepperman, disappeared from the airwaves in the late 1930s due to increased sensitivity to anti-Semitism, a similar character, Mr. Kitzel, appeared in 1946. This very popular hot dog vendor from *Mittel Europa* whose trademark sales pitch was "Peekle een the meeddle mit da mustard on top!",[134] got his laughs by mispronouncing words and transforming well-known public personalities and natural wonders into Jews: Ed Solomon (Ed Sullivan), Nat King Cohen (Nat King Cole) and Lake Shapiro (Lake Superior).[135]

Benny's wit was that of a man who stood between two worlds. It has traces of the immigrant's bewilderment at the strangeness of the new, of someone whose success has not yet brought security and acceptance.[136] At the same time, that very insecurity struck a responsive chord that made him loved even as his persona traded on the opposite. Benny's comic style had a universal appeal which would inspire, among others, future talk show hosts Jack Paar and Johnny Carson. Through them he made a lasting impression on American television.

THE BORSCHT BELT

Humor's Cauldron

A haven from the trend towards de-Semitization in the 1930s and '40s were the Jewish resorts in the Catskills mountains—the "Borscht Belt." As early as 1893, the Rand McNally Guide to the Hudson River described the Catskills town of Tannersville as "a great resort of our Israelite brethren."[137] In the following decades, the original Catskills farm/boarding houses were enlarged and updated, turned into hotels and *kukhaleyns* (literally "cook alones," where guests had their own kitchen accommodations), and eventually replaced by vast and glitzy hotel complexes with swimming pools, golf courses, seemingly endless menus (the subject of much comic commentary), and an impressive list of entertainments.

In his classic memoir, *The Borscht Belt*, the performer Joey

THE FLAGLER Hotel and Country Club, So. Fallsburg, N.Y.

Catskills hotel postcard
(Peter H. Schweitzer
Collection)

Adams recalls, "As the hotels grew, so did the complaints from the guests . . . .That's how the farmers were forced into show business. Each had to get a specialist to calm his nervous customers."[138] During the 1920s and '30s, Catskills hotels provided an intermediary station for many entertainers, as they moved from vaudeville to Broadway, and later to film, radio and television. But it was the *tumler* who gave the Catskills a unique style of entertainment. In Borscht Belt parlance, a *tumler* (one who creates commotion) was a kind of social director whose job it was, according to Adams, "to sacrifice taste, discretion, intelligence and *amour-propre* in order to keep the guests distracted."

The *tumler*'s task was to create endless diversions for the hotel guests. He led calisthenics in the morning, clowned his way through softball, tennis or the swimming pool in the afternoons, coordinated amateur theater nights in the evening, and topped off the day by dancing with the wallflowers. Eventually he evolved a few routines, most of them plagiarized from vaudeville acts: "The food at the hotel is rotten—and the portions are so small."[139] But it was in these Borscht Belt hotels that Jewish comedians could interact with audiences who shared their language and culture.[140] And it was as social director that Jewish comedians such as Danny Kaye, Jerry Lewis, and many others, got their first taste of show business.[141]

Borscht Belt audiences were notoriously tough. Failure to keep them amused could be damning. One anecdote tells of Jerry Lewis's father, Danny, bombing on stage:

> **The next morning he sat at the breakfast table very alone, conscious of hostile stares. A female voice broke the funereal quiet with an instruction to the waiter: "Give him orange juice like he gave us a show last night."[142]**

This trial by fire was a challenge, which gave rise to a humor born out of desperation. Some of it was self-directed (Jerry Lewis pouring plates of soup over his head); some of it was vulgar; but mostly it was a hyperactive, "shpritzing" style, which played upon the self-consciousness of its audiences, who had gained a foothold in American culture but remained very much aware of how close they still were to their "lowly" past.

The *tumlers* cultivated a performance style of ad-libbing, use of Yiddishisms, insults, and the illusion of one-to-one contact. They also picked up on the tradition of linguistic play and imitation that characterized vaudeville. Danny Kaye for example would demonstrate his "proficiency" in foreign languages, presenting nothing more than a torrent of nonsense syllables that sounded like German, French, or Chinese.[143] Sid Caesar presented parodies of foreign films spoken in his own brand of Catskills gibberish.[144]

By the late 1950s, the popularity of the Catskills had peaked. Cheap airfares brought the resorts of Miami within easy reach, while a strong dollar and disposable income enhanced Europe's allures. By then Catskills comedy had made its way into the mainstream, where it followed the route of an emerging medium of mass communications, television.

TELEVISION

The Return of Jewish Comics

In its infancy, television fought hard to win audiences and fill program slots. To do so it experimented with different formats. A staple of 1950s television was the comedy variety show, which replicated the vaudeville model with its repertoire of gags, short skits and improvisations. A highly successful format, which required little advance preparation time, and could be produced in front of live audiences, such shows depended on a central figure to tie the skits together, relate to the studio audience, create continuity between the program and commercials, and provide a personal signature.

This role exactly replicated the versatility of the Catskills social director and master of ceremonies, the *tumler*. Indeed, many erstwhile *tumlers* found a ready niche in early television.

Scrambling for talent to fill its prime-time slots, the new medium became an open field for Jewish comic talent. In the 1950s, Milton Berle, George Burns, Jack Benny, Georgie Jessel, Sid Caesar, Morey Amsterdam, Groucho Marx, and Phil Silvers, even veteran actors such as Menashe Skulnik, all starred in their own comedy shows.

This unprecedented prominence of Jewish comedians resulted in a phenomenon which Wallace Markfield described as the "Yiddishization of American humor." At a time when Yiddish itself was thought of as a dying language, Jewish comedians projected Yiddish right into American living rooms, and with it, into American English. Suddenly, Borscht Belt humor, with all its aggressiveness, was there for all Americans to share. Yiddish/Jewish was no longer a secret code, but, as Irving Howe observed, a "major boast," which mirrored the newly gained self-confidence of Jewish urban professionals.[145]

By far the boldest of such talent was Sid Caesar. In *Your Show of Shows* (NBC, 1950-1954), and later in *Caesar's Hour* (NBC, 1954-1957) he, along with his co-stars Imogene Coca, Carl Reiner, and Howard Morris, carried the parody of post-World War II American culture to an extreme. Caesar developed his talent as a young boy by imitating the foreign dialects of workers visiting his father's Yonkers diner, and perfected his art during his Borscht Belt years. His sketches, developed by a team of writers which included none other than Mel Brooks, Larry Gelbart, Carl Reiner, Neil Simon, Woody Allen, and Mel Tolkin,[146] explored the dark side of the emerging consensus culture, with its emphasis on social mobility, consumerism,

romance and family life. His genius for mimicry permeates "The General Dresses Up," (a sketch about a German "general" who turns out to be a doorman), as well as his parodies of contemporary Japanese, Italian and French art films, which present Japanese characters with such unlikely Yiddish names as *Gantse Mishpokhe* (Whole Family), *Gehakte Leber* (Chopped Liver), or *Shmate* (Rag), and situate a "French romance" in a restaurant called *La Fligl* (The Chicken Wing).[147]

This "Yiddishization" also emerged in a particular style of reasoning, outlook on the world, and body language. Whereas an earlier generation of performers, such as Menashe Skulnik or Ed Wynn, appeared as perpetual immigrants, at a loss with the world, Phil Silvers' Sergeant Bilko, with his schemes to remake the army into a personal business, was the *luftmentsh* reincarnate; Alan King's cynicism towards relationships and the suburban way of life assessed the cost of assimilation and social mobility; Milton Berle's, Buddy Hackett's and Don Rickles's cultivation of impropriety turned immigrants' cultural shame into taunts of those less verbally aggressive; and Jerry Lewis and Danny Kaye transformed Jewish anxiety into the bodily discomfort of the *klutz,* the misfit.

Although Jewish comedians continued to avoid explicitly Jewish impersonations, their characters were often implicitly coded as Jewish in a variety of ways: Caesar presented spoofs of archetypal middle European refugee intellectuals such as "The Professor," who, in his interviews with a reporter played by Carl Reiner, would expound his outrageous theories on such topics as sleep and mountain climbing; Wayne and Shuster, parodying the Western, introduced Tex Rorschach, the nebbishy "frontier psychiatrist (Have couch, will travel)."

> Tex: "Poor Ringo Kid, you're just an angry little boy lashing out at the world with your six gun."
> Ringo: "You trying to tell me I'm crazy?"
> Tex: "Oh, please, Ringo. We don't use words like crazy anymore. Let me simply say you are suffering from a traumatic dislocation of your emotional processes."
> Ringo: "Well, what does that mean?"
> Tex: "You're a nut. You're crazier than a cocoanut. You're *meshuga*."[148]

By the late 1950s, television sponsors increasingly sought to gain control over network programming. They honed in on the unpredictable and oftentimes explosive humor of the comedy-variety show, in which the pronounced role of the master of ceremonies and spontaneous ad-libbing came to be regarded as liabilities. Programming began to shift away from variety shows, toward the sitcom formula, which, pre-recorded and studio edited, provided less room for surprises. *Caesar's Hour* was cancelled in 1957. In 1951 Milton Berle, "Mr. Television," had signed a thirty-year contract with NBC. In 1960, he found himself banished to the program *Jackpot Bowling*, while Groucho Marx hosted *You Bet Your Life*. Game shows provided the last refuge for the mad antics of Jewish comedians.[149]

In a replay of the 1930s, proposals for new television sitcoms that were deemed "too Jewish" for the vastly expanded, and mostly mid-American television audience, were rewritten and recast. Carl Reiner's proposed show *Head of the Family*—

loosely based on his own experiences of growing up Jewish in the Bronx—was "de-Semitized." Not only was it recast with the WASP, tall Dick Van Dyke, instead of Reiner, as lead, but even its locale was changed to the American heartland. It eventually aired as the phenomenally successful *Dick Van Dyke Show*.[150] Even though Reiner was able to reintroduce some Jewish themes through the New York Jewish wiseguy character of Buddy, played by Morey Amsterdam, the marginalization of Jewish characters is obvious.

Although they no longer hosted their own programs, Jewish comedians frequently appeared as guests on variety and late night talk shows, where they could spice up the program with their outsider's irony and lack of shame. But even on late night television, pressures on stand-up comedians to keep their acts within certain limits were considerable. In his 1959 appearance on *The Steve Allen Show*, "sicknik" comedian Lenny Bruce showed visible restraint, and he recognized his incompatibility with prime time conventions. "My language," he later acknowledged, "is completely larded with hip idiom and Yiddish idiom," a style which did not appeal to the average television viewer.[151]

A famous casualty of television's trend towards normalization was Jackie Mason, whose curvilinear monologues, developed before Borscht Belt audiences, were often an elaboration on the distinction between Jews and non-Jews:

> Let me tell you something; there's not a Jew in the world who can do anything with his hands. It's a well-known fact. And why? Because a Jew was never raised

to use his hand to do anything but turn a page. To this day, a Jew can't fix a car. If a Jewish car breaks down, it's all over. He can't do nothing. Watch a Gentile car break down. In two seconds, he's under the car, on top of the car, it becomes an airplane. A Jewish car breaks down, you hear the same thing:

"It stopped."

And the wife says, "It's your fault."

The husband has an answer: "I know what it is. I know what it is. It's in the hood."

The *yenta* says, "Where's the hood?"

"I don't remember."[152]

After an infamous appearance on *The Ed Sullivan Show,* which resulted in a public falling-out with the show's host, Mason's career took a nose dive. According to the comedian

people said I was too Jewish—and I even suffered from anti-Jewish prejudice from Jews themselves. There was a profound rejection problem: the reverse discrimination of Jews against other Jews who talk like me in show business. I think they were ashamed and embarrassed about my accent, that I was somehow symbolic of the fear that Jews would be discriminated against again.[153]

It would take another generation for American Jews to feel safe enough in their middle-class existence to accept Mason's excess as a welcome reminder of a past which they once had been all too eager to leave behind.

STAND-UP COMEDY

Humor on the Edge

After a short period of "philo-Semitism," to use Irving Howe's characterization of the 1950s,[154] many Jewish comedians again found themselves outside the mainstream.[155] A new generation of college-bred comics found refuge in such night clubs as the "Bitter End" in New York City, "Second City" in Chicago and the "Hungry i" in San Francisco. Although these performers were known collectively as "sickniks" or "the sick comedians," they varied widely in their content and delivery. What comedians like Mort Sahl, Shelley Berman, Lenny Bruce, Bill Dana, Don Addams, Mike Nichols and Elaine May shared was the cynical, self-deflationary mood of the post-Korean War era. Exploring themes of social and cultural alienation, existentialism, and anti-heroism, their humor assaulted the taboos of the consensus culture of the 1950s. Not only did they satirize the American good life with its suburban values, swimming pools and patio barbecues, they also tackled the H-bomb and nuclear shelters, McCarthyism, racism, segregation, organized religion, perversion and disease.[156] Often unapologetic in their Jewishness, their routines reflected the new-found economic and social stability of American Jews. Their irreverent, urban, often jazzy style was replicated in the novels of Philip Roth, Bernard Malamud and Saul Bellow, and the cartoons of Jules Feiffer, and at times provoked vehement protests from Jewish, as well as non-Jewish audiences.

An important center of the new humor was Chicago. Shelley Berman, Mike Nichols and Elaine May were graduates from a college theater group which later became known as the Compass Players, and found their performance home in the Second City. Shelley Berman excelled in evocative portraits which captured his Chicago Jewish family and West Side neighborhood, and its pervasive sense of ambition and insecurity. His favorite format was the telephone conversation. A particularly sensitive routine is an eight-minute dialogue between himself and his father, a delicatessen owner, following his request for a loan of $100 to register for acting school in New York:

> My father makes a reasonably good living in his delicatessen selling sandwiches to the laborers in the neighborhood. And there are many laborers in this neighborhood. My father refers to laborers in a rather peculiar fashion. He calls them *goyim*. I will explain

this esoteric term. No one will be left out, I assure you. *Goyim* is plural for *goy*. *Goy* is a rather singular way of saying Gentile. As far as my father is concerned all laborers are Gentiles. Even a Jew who is a laborer is a Gentile as far as my father is concerned. He is an exceedingly narrow-minded man . . . However, in spite of his narrow-mindedness he does have some golden virtues. Among them—he makes a good living.

At the end of the dialogue, in which Berman impersonates his father's East European inflections, the father offers him the money, along with additional funds for the airfare and hotel, and closes the conversation with one request: "Listen, Sheldon. Sheldon? Don't change your name. Goodbye, Sheldon."[157]

Elaine May and Mike Nichols scrutinized the pathology of middle-class life. One routine features a rocket scientist on the telephone with his mother, who scolds him for not having called, then informs him that she's about to enter the hospital to have her nerves X-rayed. The son apologizes.

> Mother: "What's the use of talking. No, no. You're very young. Someday, someday Arthur, you'll get married. And you'll have children of your own. And honey, when you do, I only pray that they make you suffer the way you're making me. That's all I pray, Arthur. That's a mother's prayer [Weeping]."
> Son: "O.K. mom, thanks for calling."[158]

By the end of the conversation, the son has regressed to

baby talk. The routine codes the characters' Jewishness through the stereotypes of an overbearing mother and a son desperate, but unable to break the bond. Indeed, the very tension in the mother/son relationship speaks to deep-seated insecurities and guilt feelings on the part of a young generation of successful Jewish professionals, pushed by their working- and lower-middle-class parents into the relentless pursuit of social mobility, tensions that would resurface in film comedies and Jewish "How To" books a decade later.

The political nature of Mort Sahl's satire places him somewhat apart from the other "sickniks." First appearing at the "Hungry i" in 1953, Sahl aimed his sights at corporate America, the government and its various agencies. In one routine he portrayed himself as a naive reserve soldier called up during a Cold War era threat. When his commanding officer cites Russian anti-Semitism among the reasons for going to war, Sahl remarks sardonically that the Russian people were anti-Semitic before Communism and that "there's some things they can't ruin."[159]

But the most legendary of the "sick" comedians was Lenny Bruce, who assailed moral duplicity. Bruce was Jeremiah. His musings were less playful than prophetic. He attacked racism, organized religion and censorship. And he used the lingo of African American jazz musicians to code the radical thrust of his humor. He was scornful of Jewish assimilationists (he used Yiddish provocatively in his routines) and he took special delight in flaunting his Jewishness. One of his most famous routines elaborates a unique typology distinguishing "Jewish" from "*goyish.*"

I'm Jewish. Count Basie's Jewish. Ray Charles is Jewish. Eddie Cantor's *goyish.* B'nai Brith is *goyish;* Hadassah, Jewish. Marine corps—heavy *goyim,* dangerous. Koolaid is *goyish.* All Drake's Cakes are *goyish.* Pumpernickel is Jewish, and, as you know, white bread is very *goyish.* Instant potatoes—*goyish.* Black cherry soda's very Jewish. Macaroons are very Jewish—very Jewish cake. Fruit salad is Jewish. Lime jello is *goyish.* Lime soda is very *goyish.* Trailer parks are so *goyish* that Jews won't go near them.[160]

But much more biting is his satire on the origins of anti-Semitism and the calumny of deicide:

. . . you and I know what a Jew is—*One Who killed Our Lord.* I don't know if we got much press on that in Illinois . . .

Allright. I'll clear the air once and for all, and confess. Yes, we did it. I did it, my family. I found a note in my basement. It said:

"We killed him.

signed,

Morty."

And a lot of people say to me,

"Why did you kill Christ?"

I dunno . . . it was one of those parties, got out of hand, you know. We killed him because he didn't want to become a doctor, that's why we killed him.[161]

FILM COMEDY

A Choice of Heroes

On July 11,1969, *Life*'s feature story was titled: "Dusty and the Duke: A Choice of Heroes." The top half of the issue's cover was a black-and-white sketch of Dustin Hoffman, seen in profile and from a distance, wearing winter street clothes, hands in pocket, and shoulders slouched. The bottom half showed John Wayne in cowboy outfit, sketched in bright colors, his face a large frontal close-up, with teeth exposed.

Life's cover story poignantly illustrates a critical divide in American history: by the end of the 1960s, the model for the archetypal male hero wavered between two extreme poles: Wayne, "strong, decisive and nearly always a winner;" and Hoffman, the "uncertain, alienated, complex, and, by any familiar standard, loser." Wayne represented the "solid, conservative out-

Courtesy of Milton Glaser

"Dusty and the Duke: A Choice of Heroes"
(*Life*, July 11, 1969) (Kugelmass Collection)

doorsman, knowing exactly what he thinks, who he is and where he is going," Hoffman the "restless, introverted city dweller, full of questions and not at all sure what the answers are."

Dustin Hoffman had been catapulted to stardom after the success of *The Graduate* (1967), his first major film, which co-starred Anne Bancroft and earned its director, Mike Nichols, an Oscar. In the movie, Hoffman appeared as a naive college graduate who is seduced by a spoiled and bored middle-aged housewife, but falls in love with her daughter. His character represented the existential hero, whose misfit personality challenges the ethics of his upper-middle-class environment. Although there was nothing Jewish about the film's characters, Hoffman's hero bore an uncanny resemblance to a ubiquitous character in Jewish folk- and literary imagination— the schlemiel.[162]

The Graduate signalled the return of the anti-hero, and with it, representations of Jews suddenly burst upon the screen. Besides a shift in American ideals of masculinity, this new Jewish visibility owed much to the emergence of independent film production com-

George Burns and Walter Matthau in
The Sunshine Boys

panies, which were more willing to develop unconventional sto-
rylines than the major Hollywood studios. But it also rode the
tide of a more widespread ethnic revival—itself a response to
Black nationalism and other liberation movements, including

feminism and gay pride—as well as a rise of nationalism among
Jews, particularly in the wake of the 1967 War.

The two directors most credited for the reintroduction of
the Jew as comic hero to the screen are Mel Brooks and Woody

Allen. Brooks's first movie, *The Producers* (1968), featured two stock figures—the neurotic mama's boy (Gene Wilder) and the money-hungry older lecher (Zero Mostel)—in a money-making scheme that involves the production of a musical in extremely bad taste (*Springtime for Hitler,* advertised as "a gay romp with Adolph and Eva in Berchtesgaden") designed to flop instantly. The movie carried Brooks's signature as a shatterer of taboos, and invited sharp criticism from the Jewish press. But others, less offended, considered Brooks's sensibility a direct outgrowth of the Borscht Belt spirit.[163]

Mel Brooks was especially creative in spoofing American mythology—the West, Outer Space or Hollywood—and repopulating these mythic landscapes with comic Jewish, or Jewish inflected characters. Actually, the West had been a favorite site for Jewish parody since the days of Yiddish vaudeville. But in the 1970s and '80s, the cowboy, dethroned as king of the West, suddenly found flawed heroes and Yiddish spouting characters right by his side. Mel Brooks's *Blazing Saddles* (1973), a parody of the classic Hollywood Western, featured a black sheriff, played by Cleavon Little as a mixture of schlemiel and tough guy, a Dietrich-like chanteuse named "Lily Von Shtup" (Madeline Kahn), and, in a throwback to vaudeville conventions, a Yiddish speaking Indian chief, played by Mel Brooks himself, who announces upon spotting an African American family in a covered wagon, "They're darker than us!" Perhaps no line ever uttered on screen or stage better articulated the complexity of comedic African American/ Jewish mirroring or the implications of a social system in which "racial" exclusion partly enabled Jewish inclusion.

Radical re-territorialization informs the plots of much of Brooks's work, from *Young Frankenstein* (1974), a remake of the classic *The Bride of Frankenstein*, to *History of the World- Part I* (1981). But it is particularly pronounced in *Spaceballs* (1987). A take-off on *Star Wars*, the film features a dashing blond but ineffectual hero, portrayed as an archetypal *goy*, who falls in love with a space princess exhibiting all the characteristics of a Jewish American Princess, who is kidnapped, but ultimately saved through the intervention of the Yiddish accented king of a dwarf colony, and the power of "The Schwartz."

While Brooks's humor rests heavily upon a strategy of subversive de-centering, no contemporary Jewish comic more fully elaborates the schlemiel hero than Woody Allen. In his career as a writer for *Your Show of Shows*, stand-up comic, author (his "The Kugelmass Episode" won the O'Henry Award for best short story), actor and filmmaker, Allen has created feminized male heroes whose ineptness and preoccupation with *Weltschmertz* (cosmic pain) is typically counterbalanced by their ethical nature.

Like Brooks and other Jewish comic writers, "high culture" and "classics" constitute a favorite target for Allen's parodies: Ingmar Bergman's *Smiles of a Summer Night* inspired Allen's *A Midsummer Night's Sex Comedy*; *Love and Death* played out a Jewish version of Tolstoy's *War and Peace*; *Play It Again Sam* (1972), a film in which the main character, Allan Felix, tries to develop his masculinity by styling himself after Humphrey Bogart's character in *Casablanca*, spoofs the world of intellectuals. In the hope of meeting someone of the opposite sex,

Felix goes to an art museum. Spotting a woman standing in front of a Jackson Pollock, he asks what the painting means to her.

> "It re-states the negativeness of the universe. The hideous lonely emptiness of existence. Nothingness. The predicament of Man forced to live in a barren, Godless eternity like a tiny flame flickering in an immense void with nothing but waste, horror and degradation, forming a useless bleak straightjacket in a black absurd cosmos."
>
> "What are you doing Saturday night?" Felix asks.
>
> "Committing suicide," she responds.
>
> "What about Friday night?"[164]

Allen typically frames his exploration of Jewish masculinity within the context of a Jewish/goyish dialogue, in which a non-Jewish female serves as his foil. Perhaps nowhere is this dichotomy more explicit than in his Oscar-winning masterpiece *Annie Hall*. The film portrays the romance between the film's Jewish hero, Alvy Singer (Woody Allen) and its non-Jewish female lead, Annie Hall (Diane Keaton). In one sequence, the couple travel to Chippewa Falls, Wisconsin, to spend Thanksgiving with Annie's family. Seated at the dinner table which displays a giant ham, and feeling utterly out of place, (the film inserts simultaneous scenes of the two families celebrating, contrasting the quiet, well-bred middle American Halls and the loud, working-class New York Singers), Alvy notices Annie's grandmother staring at him. Imagining himself through her

eyes, he is suddenly transformed into an ultra-orthodox Jew, wearing a black caftan, hat, beard and *peyes*!

But nowhere is the profoundly ethical nature of the schlemiel more apparent than in the film *Broadway Danny Rose* (1984) where Allen, as Danny Rose, a not too successful theatrical agent (his acts include a blind xylophone player and a stuttering ventriloquist), tries to convince interior decorator Tina (Mia Farrow), one-time wife of a mafia "juice-man" and current mistress of one of his clients (an over-the-hill crooner making a come-back), to have more confidence in herself. The two discuss their respective philosophies of life—Tina's includes doing it to the other guy before he does it to you.

> Danny: This is a philosophy of life? It sounds like the screenplay of *Murder Incorporated.* That's ridiculous! No wonder you don't like yourself.
> Tina: You're the one that's living like a loser.
> Danny: Why? 'Cause I haven't made it? You see, that's the beauty of this business. That's the beauty of it. Overnight you can go from a bum to a hero. . . . Let me just say one thing. My Uncle Sidney, a man, lovely uncle, dead, completely, used to say three things. He used to say: "Acceptance, forgiveness, and love." And *that* is a philosophy of life. Acceptance, forgiveness, and love. So there is where it is.

By far the most satiric film of this period was *Goodbye Columbus* (1969). Based on a Philip Roth story, its portrayal of the doomed romance between a young community librarian

Gene Wilder in the film *The Frisco Kid* (1979) (Wisconsin Center for Film and Theater Research)

(Richard Benjamin) and the daughter of the newly prosperous Patemkin family (Ali MacGraw) explored the theme of Jewish social mobility and the cultural emptiness and false morality of the *parvenu*. The movie's most revealing scene portrays a wed-ding banquet, which fully exposes the family's social snobbery, low-class sentimentality and provides a close-up of the vulgar-ity of the guests. The scene was widely criticized for its indict-ment of American Jewry in the late 1960s, and was vilified as an "anti-Jewish joke." Commenting on the production of the scene, editor Ralph Rosenblum recalled that the two hundred extras were simply told to "behave as you would at a Jewish wedding." The result was beyond expectation:

> We were somewhat pleased with the hilarious demolition job we were pulling off on the offensive relatives that had at one time or another made us ashamed to be Jewish. But our pleasure was mitigated by guilt . . . "My God," we thought. "What have we done?"

After submitting a heavily edited version of the banquet scene to the (Jewish) executive at Paramount, however, they were rebuked for "having left out all the ethnic stuff" and ordered to recompose the scene.[165]

By the mid 1970s, Jewish film comedy, by and large, took a milder turn, characterized in particular by the comedy of Neil Simon. The most widely produced playwright of the century, Simon's theater inflected the everyday realities of the New York middle-class with a "comic plaintiff voice."[166] His work is marked by a sensitivity to the nuances of speech, body language, and class—qualities that, combined, often suggest, without ever explicitly articulating, the Jewishness of his characters. According to Stephen Whitfield, Simon once distinguished between "writing Gentile" (for example, *Barefoot in the Park*) and "writing Jewish," by which he meant that "Jewish is more than black cherry soda and rye bread," it is "martyrdom, and self-pity, and 'everything terrible happens to me.'"[167] By that rule, examples of Simon "writing Jewish" are *The Odd Couple* (1968), which in its screen version starred Jack Lemmon and Walter Matthau as two divorced men sharing a household and was later developed into a television series; and *The Sunshine Boys* (1975), starring George Burns and Walter Matthau as two cranky retired comic actors (modeled after the vaudeville team of Smith and Dale) who are coaxed into teaming up once more for a TV come-back. The role earned George Burns an Oscar.

Robert Aldrich's *The Frisco Kid* (1979) reinvoked the theme of the schlemiel transported to the West, but his reworking was more sentimental than parodic. The film starred Gene Wilder as a hapless yeshiva student in Poland, hired as a rabbi by the Jewish community of San Francisco. In his journey West, Wilder is initiated into American manhood by Harrison Ford, the rough outlaw with the golden heart. At the very moment that he demonstrates mastery of the art of gunfighting, Wilder remains true to a higher ethical code, and renounces his gun-toting masculine self. In *The Frisco Kid*'s hierarchy of heroes, as in many other Jewish film comedies, John Wayne plays second fiddle to the schlemiel.

COMMODITY CULTURE

Marking Boundaries

In their portrayals of neurotic sons, suffocating mothers, ineffectual fathers, and spoiled daughters, the film comedies of the 1960s and '70s transformed the social trajectory of American Jewry into a source of laughter. Their images of the body (in need of over-protection and prone to disease), gesture and posture (signifying guilt and insecurity), and language (argumentativeness, the tendency to overtalk, and especially the use of Yiddish) condensed the chasms of class and culture that separated an older from a younger generation. Jewishness, for a generation reared with an eye towards achievement and mobility, and bent on mastering the cultural codes of the dominant class, was defined as excess: too much talk, gesturing, food, love, expectation, and protection.

The broad-based vernacular culture which, in the 1960s, started churning out posters, books, greeting cards, board games, dolls (there is a Jewish "Barbie"), mugs and a vast array of novelty items (matzo ball beach balls, inflatable bagels, and Jewish fortune cookies proclaiming "Have we got a cookie for you! . . . the wisdom of a Jewish scholar . . . . the advice of a Jewish mother . . . the wit of Uncle Sidney . . . the chutzpa of an Aunt Fanny in every box!") elaborated on the same themes. Like the comedic film, it promoted the idea of the funniness of the Jew as innate—as an essential and inalterable characteristic of Jewish difference.

On occasion, these comic Jewish objects drew the same sort of flak as stage and print productions. In 1966, for example, two New York area Jewish businessmen produced a novelty item, "Instant Jewish." It was a small can containing powdered chicken soup, a guide to holding a bar-mitzvah in a Chinese restaurant, a registration card for a Cadillac, a guide to Jewish delicatessens and a discount shopping guide to New York City. After promoting "Instant Jewish" in a local paper, protests forced the distributors to remove the item from the shelves and no more than a hundred were ever sold.

Despite occasional objections to what some consider a slur or at least a trivialization of Judaism, the market for these items is vast, and expanding. A particularly productive genre of Jewish output is printed spoof and parody. In the 1960s, when Jewish humor began to take cognizance of Israel, and particularly after the June War of 1967, a Jewish spy named Israel Bond, appeared as Israeli agent Oy-Oy-7 in *Loxfinger*, *Matzoball* and *On the Secret Service of His Majesty, the Queen*.

Popular magazines have also been a forum for Jewish parody. *Mad* has long included spoofs on Jewish subjects, including feature-length parodies of the film *Yentl* ("Mentl") and the television sitcom *The Nanny* ("The Ninny") and a record insert featuring a song tribute to the altered Jewish body, "She Got a Nose-Job." And *The National Lampoon*'s spoof "Our Greatest Jewish Presidents" is illustrated with a Milt Gross cartoon, featuring the four men of Mt. Rushmore with scaffolding holding up their protruding noses.

But perhaps the most interesting genre of contemporary Jewish humor consists of "How To" books. A classic of this kind is Dan Greenburg's *How to Be a Jewish Mother*. First released in 1964, it quickly sold over 3 million copies in 15 editions, and is still in print, now in a glitzy, updated, 30th-anniversary edition. The book offers simple, diagrammed instructions for mastering the art of Jewish motherhood. Figure 1 presents "Proper position of hands during execution of daily sigh" and shows a woman's chubby hands crossed, the lower one holding a handkerchief. Figure V shows a 1960s vintage space capsule whose exterior is cut away to reveal a '50s-style bungalow interior. The caption reads: "Jewish mother's plan for an improved space capsule." Figure VI, accompanied by a caption which reads: "Proper outfit for taking a little sun at the beach," shows a Jewish son, wearing a jacket, tablecloth, shower clogs, hat and holding an umbrella.[168]

As a prototype for subsequent "How To" books, *How to Be a Jewish Mother* is particularly revealing. It encodes Jewishness on three intersecting axes: class, body and language. The Jewish mother is lower middle-class (witness the space capsule). And although her children are well positioned for upward mobility, the climb out of the ghetto leaves Jewish children ill at ease, their bodies insecure, unprotected, and, therefore, continually in rebellion. *The Jewish Adventurers' Club*, for example, packs its survival belt with a compass/inhaler and a medication dispenser that "includes thirty-seven known and exotic brands of antihistamines . . . ."[169]

Adult children of Jewish parents, Anna Sequoia suggests in a book of that title, waver between over-eating and dieting:

> Mark: "My theory is there's no such thing as overeating: there's only underbuying. When I shop for food, anything that I can store or freeze I buy by the case."
> Melinda: "I don't understand what the fuss is about. Anyone with a little self-discipline can be thin . . . When I've eaten too much, I just throw up."[170]

"More than anything else," Sequoia asserts, "Adult Children of Jewish Parents love *going* to doctors . . . " For convenience sake, she includes "A Short Guide to Specialty Diseases of Adult Children of Jewish Parents." The list includes: colitis, Crohn's Disease, Epstein-Barr, hypertension, asthma, hypoglycemia, shingles, herpes, depression, diabetes, urinary tract infections, constipation, anorexia, arthritis, dermatitis, hangnails and allergies, among other things, to "paying full retail price, taking public transportation . . . cheap wines."[171]

As suggested by the figure of the hand-wringing mother in Greenburg's *How to Be a Jewish Mother*, the Jewish body has its own language, an idea which is borne out by Molly Katz's *Jewish as a Second Language*, which interprets the meanings of "The Four Basic Shrugs":

> **>Incredulous** ("I was supposed to know it would rain?")
> **>Helpless** ("Me? Lift *that*?")
> **>Stymied** ("Look it up in the dictionary.")
> **>All-purpose** ("Go know.")[172]

But Jewish spoken language is as unintelligible to outsiders as Jewish body language. A standard feature in subsequent "How To" books is the (pseudo) dictionary, which explains the basic terms of "Jewish Jargon." Greenburg's pseudo-dictionary includes such terms as

> *for later*:
> (As in "Take a little spongecake *for later*") To be eaten within the next two weeks.
> *heart attack*:
> Lower middle-class coronary.
> *gratitude*:
> What a Jewish mother does not expect. [173]

In *The Jewish American Princess Handbook*'s glossary, an insiders' term as *machetonum* is explained as "Two opposing sets of parents who pretend to get along because their *kinderlach* are getting married," while the term *polyester* is translated as "What?"[174] The ubiquity of such dictionaries gives credence to the idea of a hidden Jewish language, which, according to Sander Gilman, permeates the rhetoric of Western anti-Semitism. But here that hidden language is reappropriated to form an authentic "Jewish voice."[175]

Combined, class, body and language establish a formula for connoting Jewishness perhaps best illustrated in Anna Sequoia's *The Official J.A.P. Handbook* and Debbie Lukatsky's and Sandy Barnett Toback's *The Jewish American Princess Handbook*. At first glance, these books appear to uphold the standard formula of J.A.P. jokes, contrasting the upper class aspirations of the Jewish parvenu with the crass materialism and vulgarity lying just beneath the surface.[176]

> One dark night as Muffy Hughes Fairchild strolled the cobbled avenues of the upper east side, a sense of fear and foreboding came upon her. For, in the distance there arose an unearthly glow. Closer and closer the light came and she began to shake in her Topsiders. Could this be a close encounter?
>
> As the humanoid approached, Muffy realized the glow was emanating from the profusion of gold and diamond jewelry which bedecked the female apparition. Was she from another planet? As far as Muffy was concerned she might well have been . . . she was from Long Island. The creature extended her manicured hand in a gesture of friendship and began to speak:
>
> Princess: I have been shlepping all night. This neb I was out with wanted to pick up a six-pack and go to a polo match.
>
> Muffy: Neb? Schlepp? I don't understand!
>
> Princess: I thought I'd plotz, his car was full of chazerei.
>
> Muffy: Plotz? Chazerei? If only I could communicate with her?

A closer look, however, reveals the divergence between typical J.A.P. humor (often characterized as misogynist and anti-Semitic) and these handbooks, which are anything but critical of the culture they represent. Lukatsky's and Toback's opening epigram reads "We're not spoiled, just selective." These books suggest that in the Jewish American Princess, the intersection of class, language and body acts as a depository of (a positively valued) Jewish difference. Moreover, these books police the border between Self and Other, and particularly so in regard to intermarriage—a phenomenon that poses a greater threat to Jewish women (who marry "out" less frequently) than to Jewish men. Both volumes invoke inter-ethnic dating, only to reject such liaisons as the "princess" matures and selects a more suitable, i.e., "N.J.B." (Nice Jewish Boy) or "M.O.T." (Member Of the Tribe) for marriage purposes.

While few books are as explicit in patrolling ethnic borders as the J.A.P. handbooks, most "How To" books do function as ethnic boundary markers by engaging in expositions on Jewish difference that are reminiscent of Bruce's "What's Jewish/What's Goyish" neologisms. Take, for example, *The Official J.A.P. Handbook* chart "What's JAP and What Isn't JAP."

JAP	Non-JAP
Hilton Hotels	Motel 6
corned-beef sandwiches	cucumber sandwiches
honey cake	angel cake
real diamonds	Wellington diamonds
Russian amber	Monet jewelry
skim milk	whole milk
Mt. Sinai Hospital	Bellevue Hospital
Godiva chocolates	Hershey bars[177]

Such charts articulate the "hidden" aspects of Jewish difference that not only defy assimilation, but present invisible and sometimes insurmountable cultural barriers to non-Jews. Indeed, some "How To" books are ostensibly aimed at familiarizing non-Jews with, or even acculturating them to, a world they are sometimes at a loss to comprehend, let alone function in with some degree of competence. Arthur Naiman's *Every Goy's Guide to Common Jewish Expressions*, which is basically an extensive glossary of Jewish words and concepts, in its introduction advises non-Jews that when hearing the Yiddish punchline of a joke, and feeling "once again . . . on the outside looking in, . . . and a voice within you screams 'Why wasn't I born Jewish!' . . . Screams can't make you pass for Jewish. Only this book can do that." [178]

But in this very act of translation, these books continually invoke an imaginary, albeit fluid, boundary which separates Jews from non-Jews. Katz's *Jewish as a Second Language* is intended for non-Jews marrying into Jewish families and is based on the premise that non-Jews cannot learn Yiddish. Katz advises readers not to try to improve their command of Yiddish, because faulty usage simply confirms the Jewish conviction that it defies translation, and

> that non-Jews are hopeless when they try to use it. We love to hear you deliver howlers like "When she found out she wasn't invited, she made such a big *schmatta*

> you could hear her down the street" or "Put everything on my bagel—nova, onions, the whole *schlemiel*." [179]

Besides, the true language of Jews, according to Katz, is not Yiddish, but

> the complex twists and somersaults of everyday American conversation, the swamps and thickets of behavior. It is nuances and expectations, hidden meanings and unvoiced point systems . . . wins, losses and draws in competitions you had no idea you'd entered. [180]

Interestingly, this imaginative reassertion of Jewish difference comes to the fore at the very moment when a great many Jews have achieved professional or upper-middle class status and have become part of, if not the dominant class, then at least a solid part of the mainstream of American social and cultural life. Indeed, highly eligible as marriage partners, American Jews today are confronted with an alarming rate of intermarriage, and, along with it, some "expert" demographers pessimistically predict and many Jews believe, their eventual disappearance as a distinct people. At a time when the boundaries between Jews and non-Jews seem to be dissolving, these books suggest the opposite. They articulate a Jewish difference, so firmly ensconced in class, body and language that it is sufficiently powerful to sustain a community that continues to "endure the conclusion of its perilous age." [181]

YIDDISH AS A FUNNY LANGUAGE

Talking Jewish

In Europe, Yiddish was traditionally considered a "lower" language, connected to the feminine sphere of household and marketplace, and compared unfavorably with "higher" non-Jewish languages such as German, Polish and Russian, which were associated with cosmopolitanism, elegance and civilization, or with Hebrew, the higher, masculine language of learning. By the end of the 19th century, Yiddish attained greater respectability through the creation of a high literature, press, theater, and institutions of learning, all of which travelled to, and flourished in the New World. But with the passing of the immigrant generation, the use of Yiddish increasingly became a marker of social immobility. *The Shikse's Guide to Jewish Men* describes the lower-class Jewish "tough guy" as follows:

He became a success in the underworld, as a comedian,
or in a business of his own.
The woman he marries looks like a shikse.
He stays married.
He raises his children never to forget their Jewishness.
He is deeply tied to his mother and father because he
untied himself so early.
He uses Yiddish-American words a lot: *chutzpa, shikse,
goyishe kop, hok nit kain chainik, tsimmes.*[182]

For the upwardly mobile the place of Yiddish is more conflict-
ed. As *How to Be an Extremely Reform Jew* puts it:

Yiddish also produced the Nobel Prize-winning author
Isaac Bashevis Singer and the Nobel Prize-winning
adjective, *"fahblonjet"* (meaning "hopelessly lost" or
"confused," as in "Those Extremely Reform Jews are
really fahblonjet"). Today, Yiddish lives on in Jewish
culture as an important source of bewilderment and
alienation for the Extremely Reform Jew.[183]

While Yiddish has long lost its place as the Jewish vernacular, it still exists, albeit in fragmentary form, as a language of
emotion and exaggeration. Already during the early decades of
the century, Jewish vaudeville performers used Yiddish words
and inflection as a popular comic device. At the same time, the
language served as an affirmation of ethnic origin, and rein-
forced the communal bond between performer and audience.
Since then, the comic use of Yiddish has become a mainstay of
American Jewish humor. Indeed, a strikingly common phenomenon are Yiddish glossaries (or pseudo-glossaries), which
explain basic terms with humorous definitions.

One of the earliest of such glossaries is Sam Levenson's
Basic Yiddish Lessons, which, in a mock Berlitz class, offers
lessons on Yiddish for business and dining. Levenson's strategy is to gloss Yiddish words not with direct translations but
with their meta-meaning. *Mazel,* in his interpretation, is that
which only your competitor has. In *Kosher Kalories*, the teacher
introduces his students to the "basic foods essential to the life
of the well-nourished *Litvak."*

. . .staring up at you from the center of the plate is the
world famous Jewish atomic bomb or *kneydl*. This kneydl falls in the category of the late reaction bomb. You eat
it on Saturday but it never goes off until Sunday. Sunday, you might be sitting in the movies minding your
own business . . . kneydl day is here. And wherever the
kneydl decides to go, you have to go with the kneydl.
You feel yourself slowly taking off into space. You move
in seven directions at the same time. The soup is followed by the *gebrotn* or roast, partly submerged in
shmaltz. The roast is surrounded by the Jewish K-
rations: *kashe, kugel,* and *kishke*. The only appropriate
dessert at this time would be an oxygen tank.[184]

Although dialect humor is generally associated with the cultural preferences of second generation audiences—the laughter connotes a degree of distance from immigrant parents—it

continues to be popular even among contemporary American Jews. Mel Brooks's and Carl Reiner's 2000-year-old-man speaks with a more noticeably Jewish accent with each passing year; and even the humor of *The Nanny*'s Fran, who speaks a shrill, nasal, and lower-class Queens dialect, speckled with Yiddishisms (in contrast to the upper-class British accent of her boss, Mr. Sheffield), stands in marked contrast to its '70s precursor, *Rhoda*, whose Jewish characters betrayed hardly a trace of dialect other than their New York cynicism. In contemporary Jewish humor, Yiddish inflected English or "Yinglish" (either through words, syntax or intonation) emerges as the voice of the authentic Jewish self.[185]

THE CONTEMPORARY SCENE

Too Jewish?

Rhoda signalled the successful return of Jewish lead characters to television. More often than not, *(thirtysomething*'s Michael Steadman proved an exception to the rule), they are cast as comic types, such as *Northern Exposure*'s Joel Fleischman, *Mad About You*'s Paul and *The Nanny*'s Fran, a feature which is even more pronounced when they appear as supporting characters (*thirtysomething*'s Melissa Steadman, *Murphy Brown*'s Miles Silverberg, and *The Nanny*'s Sylvia and Yetta).

Echoing complaints from the early decades of the century, these comic Jewish types at times provoke criticism for their demeaning and inauthentic representation of "real" Jews. In a 1996 *New York Times* editorial, columnist Frank Rich lamented:

When American Jews are portrayed on TV, they're most likely to embody urban Jewish-American culture rather than Judaism, a la *Seinfeld*—or to uphold traditional caricatures, like *The Nanny*.[186]

Responding to a *Los Angeles Times* review which charged *The Nanny* with offering a "demeaning depiction of Jewish womanhood," Fran Drescher, the show's creator and star, retorted that if the author of the article

was offended by someone like Fran Fine, simply because her mother has plastic slipcovers and speaks with a strong New York accent, [that] suggests that she is a victim of post-World War II culture, which says that the only good Jew is an assimilated Jew.[187]

Fran Drescher's rebuttal reflects a significant trend in American-Jewish humor. The ethnic assertiveness of post-1960s American culture brought Jewish characters once again center stage. But their difference, at least initially, was marked as an excess to which they were reluctantly bound and which they struggled tirelessly to cast off. Rhoda felt herself a captive to her mother's constant intrusions, and did all she could to prevent herself from turning into the person from whom she desperately wanted to separate—her own mother. Even the more lovable heroine of *How to Be a Jewish Mother* is excessive in her doting, and one can only fear the results as (or if) her children mature.

By the 1990s, such excess still functions as a strategy of comic representation of Jewishness, but its valuation has changed. Whereas Rhoda's and Dan Greenburg's mothers curtailed their children's sexuality, *The Nanny*'s Sylvia exudes sensuality. Her daughter, Fran, turns to her for consolation, and the cultural continuity that exists between them is apparent. Excess here is not a mark of shame, its staging a way for a succeeding generation to distinguish itself from a preceding one. It is, rather, an icon of identity.[188] Rhoda's pursuit of self-actualization, her struggle to cast off parental and other ethnic bonds reveals the essential me-centered modernism of '70s television. *The Nanny* is not only post-modern (the show's style is by self-admission a parody of a classic sitcom), it is also post-feminist (Fran has no career goals other than to marry her boss and raise his children) and post-ethnic (Jewish is a style of speech and consumption rather than a community or code of behavior). *The Nanny*'s excess, like that of Jackie Mason, Buddy Hackett or Mel Brooks, has become a Jewish version of "camp." Its rhetoric is reminiscent of the "outings" of gay liberation.

Indeed, playing on the strategy of "outing," *Saturday Night Live*'s Adam Sandler enumerates some of the many famous Jews in show business in his hit single "The Hanukkah Song." Perhaps the most poignant stanza is the following: "Some people think that Ebenezer Scrooge is [Jewish]. Well, he's not. But I'll tell you who is. All Three Stooges." Taking Ebenezer Scrooge from Dickens's *Christmas Carol*, a character easily associated with the most insidious anti-Semitic portrayal of Jews as greedy scoffers of the Christmas spirit, Sandler exposes Scrooge for what he is—a Gentile—and then flaunts the Jewishness of one of the most beloved and "lowest" comedy teams in the history of American entertainment.

The comic Jew has come a long way since he first appeared on the American stage. A century ago he mocked the foibles of fellow Jews and prodded them to move more quickly along the road of acculturation. But here is travesty in defense of the "race." The comic Jew's excess has become a badge of pride, and his (or her) laughter celebrated as a distinctive Jewish voice.

ACKNOWLEDGMENTS

The curators would like to acknowledge the following individuals for their help in collecting and interpreting the material in this exhibition: Mark Akgulian, Zachary Baker, Michael Corenthal, Shifra Epstein, Marc Fields, Krisza Fisher, Bob Freedman, Mel Gordon, Grace Grossman, Mark Hurvitz, Jim Leary, Sharon Rivo, Irv Saposnik, Chuck Schaden, Dan Sharon, Peter H. Schweitzer, Judith Summerfield, Ken Vogel, Marek Web, Olga Weiss, Paul Wesolowski and the exhibition research staff of the Spertus Museum.

The curators are grateful to the following institutions for their cooperation: Academy of Motion Pictures Arts and Sciences in Los Angeles, American Jewish Archives in Cincinnati, American Jewish Historical Society in Waltham, Mass., Asher Library of the Spertus Institute of Jewish Studies, Chicago Jewish Historical Society, Museum of Broadcast Communications in Chicago, Museum of the City of New York, Museum of Television and Radio in New York, National Center for Jewish Film in Waltham, Mass., National Museum of American History in Washington D.C., New York Public Library for the Performing Arts at Lincoln Center, Skirball Museum in Los Angeles, Theater Arts Collection of the Harry Ransom Humanities Research Center of the University of Texas at Austin, Wisconsin Center for Film and Theater Research, YIVO Institute's Archives and Library.

The curators wish to thank the following institutions for their generous support: Bernard and Audre Rapoport Fellowship in American Jewish Studies at the American Jewish Archives in Cincinnati, course development fund of the Center for Jewish Studies at the University of Wisconsin-Madison, Spertus Institute of Jewish Studies, University of Wisconsin-Madison's Sabbatical Program, University of Wisconsin-Madison's Institute for Research on the Humanities.

NOTES

1. Cited in Elliott Oring, "The People of the Joke: On the Conceptualization of Jewish Humor." *Western Folklore* 42 (1983), p261.

2. Leslie Fiedler, "The Jew as Mythic American," *Ramparts*, Vol. 2, no.2, (Autumn 1963), pp34–35.

3. The same concept is elaborated in Ruth R. Wisse's study of the place of the schlemiel in Jewish literature, *The Schlemiel as Modern Hero* (Chicago: University of Chicago Press, 1971).

4. Indeed, as Stephen Whitfield argues, humor is *"Cosa nostra, unzer shtick, our thing,"* a way of marking Jewish difference. Stephen Whitfield, "Laughter in the Dark: Notes on American-Jewish Humor," *Midstream*, (February 1978), p48.

5. Cited in Elliott Oring, "The People of the Joke: On the Conceptualization of a Jewish Humor." *Western Folklore* 42 (1983), p261.

6. Ibidem.

7. There exist a few German collections of Jewish humor that date from the early 19th century, mostly a German Jewish response to the cultural peculiarities of East European Jews migrating to Berlin and Vienna. See Sander Gilman, *Jewish Self-Hatred: Anti-Semitism and the Hidden Language of the Jews* (Baltimore: Johns Hopkins University Press, 1986), pp257–258.

8. Hermann Adler, "Jewish Wit and Humour," *The Nineteenth Century*, Vol. XXXIII, no. 193, (1893), pp457–458. See Dan Ben-Amos, "The 'Myth' of Jewish Humor," *Western Folklore* 32 (1973).

9. Abraham Isaacs, *Stories From the Rabbis* (New York: Bloch Publishing Co., 1928), p7; p9.

10. Oring, "The People of the Joke," p265.

11. Ibidem, p267–268.

12. Ibidem, p268.

13. Adler, p458.

14. Ben-Amos, p112.

15. Ibidem, pp115–117.

16. Sigmund Freud, *Jokes and Their Relation to the Unconscious* (tr.;ed. James Strachey) (New York: W.W. Norton & Company, 1960), pp64–65.

17. Benny Bell, "Blessing the Bride." *Kosher Comedy*, Zion Records, 1960.

18. Leo Fuchs, *"Galitzianer Badchen." The Best of Yiddish Vaudeville*, Banner Records.

19. Jennie Goldstein, "Here Is the Bride, But Where Is the Groom?" *The Yiddish Comedienne*. While Goldstein's parodies make frequent use of sexual innuendo, others, particularly such night club comediennes as Sophie Tucker, Pearl Williams and Belle Barth, were much more blatant. Tucker performed spicy songs such as "Make Him Say Please" or "Never Let the Same Dog Bite You Twice," and the album covers of stand-up comediennes Pearl Williams and Belle Barth feature come-ons and disclaimers such as "unsexpurgated!" "Sinsational!" or "Censored," "Not For Air Play," and "For Adults Only."

20. Cited in Joseph Telushkin, *Jewish Humor: What the Best Jewish Jokes Say About the Jews* (New York: William Morrow and Company, 1992).

21. Elliott Oring. "Jokes and the Discourse on Disaster," *Journal of American Folklore* 100, no. 399 (July–September 1987), p15.

22. John Murray Cuddihy, *The Ordeal of Civility: Freud, Marx, Lévi-Strauss, and the Jewish Struggle with Modernity* (New York: Basic Books, 1974).

23. W.E.B. Du Bois, *The Souls of Black Folk* (New York: Signet Classics, 1969), p45.

24. The shared sensibilities in Jewish American and African American humor are worth an in-depth exploration, which might suggest a more sympathetic interpretation of the meaning of the use of blackface by Jewish comedians than some contemporary critics allow for. See, for example, Michael Rogin, *Blackface, White Noise: Jewish Immigrants in the Hollywood Melting Pot* (Berkeley: University of California Press, 1996).

25. For a discussion of the functions of ethnic humor and a critique of functional theories see Mahadev L. Apte, *Humor and Laughter: An Anthropological Approach* (Ithaca: Cornell University Press, 1985), pp140–148.

26. Freud, pp111–112.

27. When told by members of the dominant group, such jokes typically poke fun at the minority group's actual or reputed deviance from normative culture (language, dress, hygiene and ethics). Indeed, the very point of such jokes is to reinforce group boundaries by ascribing deviant characteristics to outsiders. See Christie Davis, "Ethnic Jokes, Moral Values and Social Boundaries," *The British Journal of Sociology* 33, no. 3, (Sept. 1982), p400.

28. Elliott Oring makes this point in his study of the jokes that followed the Challenger disaster, "Jokes and the Discourse on Disaster." According to this analysis the jokes conjoined the unspeakable world of the mutilation of human bodies to the images of destruction repeatedly broadcast over the media. They forced us to confront what lay behind television's images.

29. See Alan Dundes, "Auschwitz Jokes" and "The Jewish American Princess and the Jewish American mother in American Jokelore," in Alan Dundes, *Cracking Jokes: Studies of Sick Humor Cycles and Stereotypes* (Berkeley: Ten Speed Press, 1986), pp19–38; 62–81. See David A. Harris and Izrail Rabinovich, *The Jokes of Oppression: The Humor of Soviet Jews* (Northvale, N.J.: Jason Aronson,1988).

30. See "Introduction," in Barbara Babcock, ed. *The Reversible World: Symbolic Inversion in Art and Society* (Ithaca: Cornell University Press, 1978), pp13–36.

31. Gilbert Seldes, *The Seven Lively Arts* (New York: Harper and Brothers, 1924), p200. Irving Howe saw this "demonic" breaking loose as the source of Jewish entertainers' affinity with black entertainers (an affinity that has substantially shaped American popular song.)

32. Irving Howe, *World Of Our Fathers: The Journey of the East European Jews to America and the Life they Found and Made* (New York: Simon and Schuster, 1976), pp566–567.

33. Stephen J. Whitfield, "The Distinctiveness of American Jewish Humor," *Modern Judaism* Vol 6, no. 3, (October 1986), pp251–252.

34. Gilles Deleuze and Felix Guattari, *Kafka: Toward a Minor Literature. Theory and History of Literature*, Vol. 30 (Minneapolis: University of Minnesota Press, 1986).

35. Whitfield, p252.

36. Allan Sherman, *A Gift of Laughter: The Autobiography of Allan Sherman* (New York: Atheneum, 1965), pp245–246.

37. Ibidem, p13.

38. David A. Harris and Izrail Rabinovich, p16.

39. In some Soviet jokes, the philosophical dimension vies for dominance with the political implications:

An East German, a West German, and a Jew were sitting on a plane. God came to them and gave each one the chance to make a wish.

"That there should only be a world without fascism," said the East German.

"That there should only be a world without Communism," said the West German.

"Excuse me, God, but will those two wishes be fulfilled?" asked the Jew.

"Yes, indeed," replied God.

"In that case, God, a cup of tea would be nice."

Ibidem, pp113–114.

40. See, for example, Steve Lipman, *Laughter in Hell: The Use of Humor during the Holocaust* (Northvale, N.J.: Jason Aronson, 1991).

41. Stephen J. Whitfield, "The Distinctiveness of American Jewish Humor" *Modern Judaism* Vol 6, no. 3, (October 1986), p250.

42. For a study of dialect humor, see Richard M. Dorson, "Jewish-American

Dialect Stories on Tape," in Raphael Patai, *et al.* eds., *Studies in Biblical and Jewish Folklore* (Bloomington: Indiana University Press, 1960), pp111–174.

43. Dundes, pp126–127.

44. Mickey Katz, *Simcha Time: Mickey Katz Plays Music for Weddings, Bar Mitzvahs and Brisses,* World Pacific/Capitol Records Inc. CDP 7243 8 30453 2 7 .

45. "Wit and Humor," *Universal Jewish Encyclopedia,* p545; Adler, p459.

46. "Wit and Humor," p546.

47. Adler, p457.

48. E. Lifschutz, "Merry Makers and Jesters Among the Jews," *Yivo Annual of Jewish Social Science,* Vol VII, (1952), pp43–83.

49. Alfred Sendrey, *The Music of the Jews in the Diaspora up to 1800* (New York: Thomas Yoseleff, 1970), pp369–372.

50. Joseph Dorinson, "Jewish Humor: Mechanism for Defense, Weapon for Cultural Affirmation," *The Journal of Psychohistory* 8, no. 4, (Spring 1981), p448.

51. Nathan Ausubel, *Treasury of Jewish Folklore* (New York: Crown, 1968), p338.

52. Wisse, pp10–11.

53. Dorinson, p448.

54. Wisse, pp10–12.

55. Sig Altman, *The Comic Image of the Jew: Explorations of a Pop Culture Phenomenon* (Rutherford: Fairleigh Dickinson University Press, 1971), p141.

56. Quoted in Freud, *Jokes and Their Relation to the Unconscious,* p16. Heine was famous for his witticisms. At a Paris *salon* frequented by financial kingpins and their deferential entourage, a friend of Heine observed, "Look at the way the nineteenth century is worshipping the Golden Calf!" "Oh, he must be older than that by now!," Heine is supposed to have responded by way of correction. On his deathbed, when a priest reminded him of God's mercy and forgiveness, Heine's rather disparaging answer was, "Bien sûr qu'il me pardonnera: c'est son métier [Of course he'll forgive me: that's his job]." Quoted in Freud, pp47–48; p114.

57. Wisse, pp25–40.

58. Ibidem, p55.

59. David Everitt, "The Man Behind the Chutzpah of Master Sgt. Ernest Bilko." *The New York Times*, Sunday, April 14, 1996, sec.H, p33.

60. "Rosenzweig, Gerson," *Encyclopedia Judaica,* Vol 14, (Jerusalem: Keter, 1992), p303.

61. Translation Kapelye, *Chicken* (Shanachie 21007).

62. Lee Tully, *"Litvak un Galitz,"* *Seltzer on the Rocks.*

63. "The Yiddisher Cowboy" was also the title of two silent movies, released in 1909 and 1911. See Patricia Erens, *The Jew in American Cinema* (Bloomington: Indiana University Press, 1984), pp38–39.

64. Ronald Sanders, "The American Popular Song," in Douglas Villiers, ed. *Next Year in Jerusalem: Portraits of the Jew in the Twentieth Century* (New York: Viking Press, 1976), p202.

65. Mark Slobin, "From Vilna to Vaudeville: Minikes and 'Among the Indians,'" *The Drama Review*, 24, no. 3, (September 1980).

66. The term "potato Yiddish" is referred to by Nahma Sandrow, "A Little Letter to Mamma: Traditions in Yiddish Vaudeville," in Myron Matlaw, ed., *American Popular Entertainment* (Westport, Conn.: Greenwood Press, 1977), p95.

67. The Barton Brothers, *"Tsuris,"* Jewish Comedy Songs, Apollo 475.

68. De Lux Records #116.

69. *Menashe Skulnik/20th Century Yiddish Humor,* Leisure Time Music #154CD.

70. Sandrow, pp87–95.

71. Michel Rosenberg, "Getzel in the Shnipashoker Society," *The Best of Yiddish Vaudeville and Michel Rosenberg,* Leisure Time Music LTM 157CD.

72. Unidentified clipping, Molly Picon Scrapbooks, Box 46, American Jewish Historical Society, Waltham, Mass.

73. Unidentified newspaper clipping, Molly Picon Collection of Scrapbooks, Box 46, American Jewish Historical Society, Waltham, Mass.

74. Jim Hoberman, *Bridge of Light: Yiddish Film Between Two Worlds* (New York: Museum of Modern Art/ Schocken, 1991), p65.

75. Ronald W. Snyder, *The Voice of the City: Vaudeville and Popular Culture in New York* (New York: Oxford University Press, 1989), p110.

76. L. Marc Fields, "The Bowery with Weber and Fields." *City Lore* Vol 5, (1995–96), p2.

77. Felix Isman, *Weber and Fields: Their Tribulations, Triumphs and Associates* (New York: Boni and Liveright, 1924), p83.

78. Armond Fields and L. Marc Fields, *From the Bowery to Broadway: Lew Fields and the Roots of American Popular Theater* (New York: Oxford University Press, 1993), ppxiii–xiv.

79. Howe, p402.

80. Albert F. McLean, "US Vaudeville and the Urban Comics," *Theater Quarterly* 1, no. 4, (Oct–Dec. 1971), p48.

81. *Hebrew Jokes*, no. 2, (New York: Wehman Bros., n.d.), p6.

82. Ibidem, p8.

83. Quoted in Paul Distler, *The Rise and Fall of the Racial Comics in American Vaudeville*, unpublished dissertation, (Tulane University 1963), p207.

84. Joe Hayman, *Twenty Different Adventures of Cohen on the Telephone and Other Different Samples of Hebrew Humour* (London: Austin Rogers & Co., 1927), pv.

85. Ibidem, p9.

86. Michael G. Corenthal, *Cohen on the Telephone: A History of Jewish Recorded Humor and Popular Music 1892–1942* (Milwaukee: Yesterday's Memories, 1984), p7.

87. Howe, p562.

88. *Chicago Israelite* May 10, 1913, Esther W. Natkin Collection, Folder 8, Chicago Jewish Archives.

89. Howe, p405.

90. Thomas Cripps, "The Movie Jew as an Image of Assimilation," *Journal of Popular Film*, 4, no. 3, (1975), p201.

91. James F. Hanley, "Abie's Irish Rose" (New York: Shapiro, Bernstein and Co., 1923).

92. Howe, p557.

93. Douglas Gilbert, *American Vaudeville: Its Life and Times* (New York: Whittlesey House, 1940), pp288–289; Howe, p562.

94. Howe, p563.

95. Sanders, pp188–189.

96. Howe, p563; Stefan Kanfer, *A Summer World* (New York: Farrar, Strauss and Giroux, 1989), p130.

97. Stefan Kanfer, "The Buckle on the Borscht Belt," *Gentleman's Quarterly*, (August 1985), p201.

98. Joe Smith, "Dr. Kronkhite Revisited," in Myron Matlaw, ed., p90.

99. Milt Gross, *Nize Baby* (New York: George H.Doran Company, 1926), p44.

100. "As I See Myself and Others," *The Jewish Tribune*, June 12, 1925, Fanny Brice scrapbook, New York Public Library at Lincoln Center.

101. Words and music by Edgar Leslie and Irving Berlin, "Sadie Salome Go Home!" (New York: Ted Snyder Co., 1909).

102. Ziegfeld engaged Brice for the 1910 Follies to do two numbers: an Irving Berlin "Yiddish dialect" song, "Goodbye, Becky Cohen," and "Lovey Joe," a so-called "coon song". Fanny interpreted the songs in an exaggerated Jewish and Southern dialect, deliberately slurring her lines and singing her "coon" song in a suggestive manner. The routine was a showstopper. See Stanley Green, *The Great Clowns of Broadway* (New York: Oxford University Press, 1984), p7.

103. Ibidem, p4.

104. *The Jewish Tribune*, June 12, 1925 (NYPL-LC).

105. Green, p4.

106. Ibidem, p3.

107. Ibidem, p12.

108. Henry Jenkins, *What Made Pistachio Nuts? Early Sound Comedy and the Vaudeville Aesthetic* (New York: Columbia University Press, 1992), p175.

109. Molly Picon, with Jean B. Grillo, *Molly! An Autobiography* (New York: Simon and Schuster, 1980), p63.

110. Howe, p562.

111. Jenkins, p173.

112. Ibidem, pp172–184.

113. Ibidem, p147.

114. Ruth Perlmutter, "The Melting Plot and the Humoring of America: Hollywood and the Jew," *Film Reader* 5, (1982), p252.

115. Harpo Marx (with Rowand Barber), *Harpo Speaks* (Kent: Coronet Books, 1978), p19.

116. Wes D. Gehring, *Groucho and W.C. Fields: Huckster Comedians* (Jackson: University of Mississippi, 1995), p160.

117. Cripps, p202.

118. Henry Popkin, "The Vanishing Jew of Our Popular Culture," *Commentary*, (July 1952), p49; Howe p567.

119. Kanfer, *A Summer World*, p157.

120. Popkin, p46.

121. Ben Hecht, *Guide for the Bedevilled* (New York: Charles Scribner's Sons, 1944), pp208–209.

122. Sam Levenson, "The Dialect Comedian Should Vanish," *Commentary*, (August 1952), pp168–169.

123. Lizabeth Cohen, *Making a New Deal: Industrial Workers in Chicago, 1919–1939* (New York: Cambridge University Press, 1990), pp133–135.

124. Cary O'Dell, "Radio's Beloved Goldbergs: the Rise of Gertrude Berg." *Nostalgia Digest*, (Oct–Nov, 1993), p4.

125. Linda Martin and Kerry Segrave, *Women in Comedy* (Secaucus N.J: Citadel Press), p161.

126. Ibidem, p161.

127. O'Dell, p5.

128. Ibidem, p6.

129. Martin and Segrave, p163.

130. Larry Gelbart, "Foreword," in *Jack Benny: The Radio and Television Work* (New York: Harper Perennial, 1991), p7.

131. Willliam A. Henry III, "Mr. Benny and America—The Long Romance," in *Jack Benny: The Radio and Television Work*, p16; Peter W. Kaplan, "Jack Benny: Our Town, His Show," in *Jack Benny: The Radio and Television Work*, p43.

132. Henry, p5.

133. Ibidem, p7.

134. Ron Simon and Rich Conaty, "The Character Behind the Man," in *Jack Benny: The Radio and Television Work*, p51.

135. Arthur Wertheim, *Radio Comedy* (New York: Oxford University Press, 1979), p327.

136. Henry, p11.

137. Howe, p215.

138. Kanfer, "The Buckle on the Borscht Belt," p147.

139. Joey Adams as quoted in Ibidem, p147.

140. Kanfer, *A Summer World*, p130.

141. Kanfer, "The Buckle on the Borscht Belt," p147.

142. Ibidem, p201.

143. Kanfer, *A Summer World*, p163.

144. Ibidem, p163.

145. Howe, p569.

146. Wallace Markfield, "The Yiddishization of American Humor," *Esquire*, LXIV, no. 4, (October 1965), p114; David Marc, *Comic Visions: Television Comedy and American Culture* (Boston: Unwin Hyman, 1989), p87.

147. Markfield, p114.

148. Wayne and Shuster, "Frontier Psychiatrist," Columbia CS 8231.

149. Marc, pp88–89.

150. Ibidem, pp110–111.

151. Ibidem, p76.

152. Jackie Mason with Ken Gross, *Jackie, Oy! Jackie Mason from Birth to Rebirth* (Boston: Little, Brown and Company, 1988), pp261–262.

153. Quoted in Sander Gilman, *The Jew's Body* (Routledge: New York, 1991), p27.

154. Howe, p568.

155. Marc, p88.

156. Kenneth Allsop, "Those American Sickniks," *The Twentieth Century*, Vol. 170, (July 1961), p98.

157. Shelley Berman, *Outside Shelley Berman*, Verve Records MG V –15007.

158. "Mother and Son." *An Evening with Mike Nichols and Elaine May*. Mercury Records OCM2200.

159. *Mort Sahl at the Hungry i*. Verve Records MG V 15012.

160. John Cohen, ed., *The Essential Lenny Bruce* (New York: Ballantine, 1967), pp41–42.

161. Ibidem, p40.

162. See Wisse.

163. In the Borscht Belt, one critic wrote "a Jewish comedian can assume a Nazi role as a temporarily shocking point of departure to arouse black laughter in his audience." Quoted in Patricia Erens, p267.

164. Condensed from Whitfield, "The Distinctiveness of American Jewish Humor," p254.

165. Erens, p275.

166. Marc, p100

167. Stephen Whitfield, "Laughter in the Dark: Notes on American-Jewish Humor." *Midstream*, (February 1978), pp52–53.

168. Dan Greenburg, *How to Be a Jewish Mother* (New York: Signet, 1967), p75.

169. Bruce Selitz, *et al*, *The Jewish Adventurers' Club* (New York: Dell, 1987), p82.

170. Anna Sequoia, *Adult Children of Jewish Parents* (New York: Crown, 1993), p56.

171. Ibidem.

172. Molly Katz, *Jewish as a Second Language* (New York: Workman Publishing, 1991), p25.

173. Greenburg, pp90–91.

174. Anna Sequoia, *The Official J.A.P. Handbook* (New York: Signet, 1982), pp142–143.

175. Gilman, *The Jew's Body*, pp1–37.

176. Debbie Lukatsky and Sandy Barnett Toback, *The Jewish American Princess Handbook* (Arlington Heights, Ill.: Turnbull & Willoughhby, 1982), p139.

177. Sequoia, *The Official J.A.P. Handbook*, p23.

178. Arthur Naiman, *Every Goy's Guide to Common Jewish Expressions* (New York: Ballantine Books, 1987), ppix–x. The volume consists of an extensive and well done glossary of Jewish words and concepts interspersed with amusing and sometimes politically charged commentary. Under the heading "mensch, " Naiman writes:

"You don't have to be well known, or even exceptional (except in your menschlichkeit), to be a mensch, but the examples I'll give of mensches will be famous people, because otherwise you won't know who I'm talking about. Martin Luther King was a mensch. Albert Einstein was a mensch. Emma Goldman was a mensch. Salvadore Allende was a mensch. Malcolm X was a mensch. Joan Baez is a mensch. Robert Redford is a mensch. And, if you ask me, Abbie Hoffman is a mensch. (This is, needless to say, a partial—as well as a partisan—list)," pp93-94.

179. Katz, p.12.

180. Ibidem.

181. Charles Silberman, *A Certain People* (New York: Simon and Schuster, 1985), p4.

182. Marsha Richman and Katie O'Donnel, *The Shikse's Guide to Jewish Men* (New York: Bantam, 1978), p17.

183. David M. Bader, *How to Be an Extremely Reform Jew* (New York: Avon Books, 1994), p9.

184. Sam Levenson, "Basic Yiddish Lesson II." In his *Meet the Folks*, the comedian Sam Levenson includes a section entitled "A Guide to Basic Yiddish." The definitions include:

DIE BUBBEH A pensioned-off baby-sitter
DER ZADEH Grandchild's press agent
TSORRES Something you get from children
NOCHES Something you get from grandchildren
Sam Levenson, *Meet the Folks* (New York: Citadel Press, 1962), pp117–122.

185. The use of Jewish dialect, according to Gilman, in Christian mythology was seen as evidence of Jewish corruption, and in modern racial theories of anti-Semitism interpreted as demonstrating the Jewish inability to master normal, i.e., non-Jewish bourgeois language and culture. See Gilman, *The Jew's Body*, pp1–37.

186. Frank Rich, "TV's New Jew," *New York Times*, Saturday, November 23, 1996, p17.

187. Quoted in Andy Meisler, "By Being All Wrong, She's Also Just Right," *New York Times*, December 18, 1994, Section 2, p47.

188. The concept of "Too Jewish" formed the theme of a recent exhibition at the Jewish Museum in New York. For a review, see Michael Kimmelman, "Jewish Artists Explore Notions of 'Too Jewish,'" *New York Times*, Section B, March 8, 1996, p1. In fact, a young generation of African American comedians, including Richard Pryor, Eddie Murphy, Arsenio Hall and Whoopi Goldberg, in their humor consciously evoke stereotypical images of Blacks that have been the focus of ridicule and de-humanization by white culture—sometimes fuelling protests within African American communities themselves.